CREATING &
DELIVERING
YOUR VALUE
PROPOSITION

CREATING & DELIVERING YOUR VALUE PROPOSITION

Managing customer experience for profit

CINDY BARNES, HELEN BLAKE, DAVID PINDER

KOGAN PAGE

London and Philadelphia

First published in Great Britain and the United States in 2009 by Kogan Page Limited

120 Pentonville Road
London N1 9JN
United Kingdom
www.koganpage.com

525 South 4th Street, #241
Philadelphia PA 19147
USA

© Cindy Barnes, Helen Blake and David Pinder, 2009

Specific © of the models and methodology in this book relating to The Value Proposition Builder™ and The Value Pyramid™ belong to Cindy Barnes and Helen Blake – Futurecurve/ Greener Consulting Ltd, 2009

The right of Cindy Barnes, Helen Blake and David Pinder to be identified as the authors of this work has been asserted by them in accordance with the Copyright, Designs and Patents Act 1988.

ISBN 978 0 7494 5512 5

British Library Cataloguing-in-Publication Data

A CIP record for this book is available from the British Library.

Library of Congress Cataloging-in-Publication Data

Barnes, Cindy, 1961–
    Creating and delivering your value proposition : managing customer experience for profit / Cindy Barnes, Helen Blake, David Pinder.
        p. cm.
    ISBN 978-0-7494-5512-5
    1. Customer relations. 2. Value. 3. Value added. I. Blake, Helen, 1962– II. Pinder, David, 1945– III. Title.
    HF5415.5.B36823 2009
    658.8'12--dc22

To our contributors, family and friends for their endless
support and understanding, especially:

Peter Barnes and Tony & Bertha Gale. CB
Bill Blake and Graeme & Joan Lee. HB
Angela Pinder and John Frazer-Robinson
(who recognized the customer imperative before
anyone else I know). DP

Contents

List of Figures

List of Tables

Acknowledgements

The world is changing, as are notions of value. Senior executives we have worked with have expressed increasing frustration with the inability to capture and harness valuable customer experiences... profitably. As we've wrestled with this issue extensively in large and small organizations, so our own thinking has been refined and crystallized though working with hundreds of talented and insightful people around the world who have given freely and generously of their time.

Any book is the child of numerous authors, many of whom may not even be aware of the influence they have made. Our influencers include all our customers and clients who, over the years, have helped us learn about true value.

Particular thanks must go, however, to those we are categorically able to recognize and thank for their direct contributions to our efforts. Neil Rackham, the world-renowned sales guru, has provided ongoing support and encouragement, read early drafts and provided advice and helpful suggestions, all with an immense generosity of time and spirit. We would also like to thank Beth Rogers, from the University of Portsmouth Business School, who has given freely of her time and guidance, and helped us with case studies. Sarah Cook provided counsel on book writing and has given us valuable introductions. Howard Murray has been a great source of sound advice and useful models, and Garri Wiest has helped with psychological insights linking emotions with the customer experience.

Sincere thanks also go to John Woodget, Jonathan Rose, Darrell Jordan-Smith, Bob Scott and Ann Sinclair for their time and thoughtful contributions.

Particular thanks must go to Annie Knight at Kogan Page. She has patiently supported and helped our efforts.

Suzi McGhee prepared, corrected and coordinated the manuscript, created the illustrations and generally kept us on track. We couldn't have done this without her.

Finally, we'd like to thank Mary Pasby, to whom we owe a great debt of gratitude. Mary brought her years of experience in sales and marketing to bear on this book and convinced us to edit significant elements for the benefit of the reader. We couldn't have done this without her all-round marvellousness.

Introduction

The term 'value proposition' is used ubiquitously in business today and its original meaning has been dissipated into vague sales and marketing notions that are a million miles away from its intended meaning and use. It is often used to mean benefits, offering, unique selling point (USP) or differentiation, and is also generally regarded as the preserve of sales and marketing and not linked to an organization's strategy.

We felt it was time to address these misconceptions and clarify what a value proposition is and what it isn't. Why you need value propositions to be profitable in business, or successful as a not-for-profit organization. And, crucially, how you build value propositions and how to use them. Although we talk about customers in the book, we don't refer solely to external customers, as everyone in the organization will have a customer. Similarly, value propositions are not just about selling. They can be used, for example, by a purchasing function to help select a supplier. Value propositions are great alignment tools and that is one of the key tenets of this book – alignment.

Another key theme is customer experience. Customer experience, in its broadest view, is hailed by many to be the next competitive battleground. What seems missing to date is how to use customer experience in a repeatable way and harness it for profit. By focusing on superior customer experience, organizations can create savings. Rather than focusing on what customers do and don't value, you focus instead on those things that customers value and that make you a profit.

We demonstrate in this book how creating value propositions is the perfect methodology for corralling and then harnessing customer experience. Since customer experience is closely allied to emotions, this model is particularly relevant to services sectors where relationships are key.

Who should read this book

We intend this book to be a practical guide for chief executive officers (CEOs), strategy officers, chief marketing officers (CMOs), chief sales officers (CSOs), customer experience heads, customer service heads, managing partners, lead consultants, directors-general, directors and assistant directors.

We aim the book primarily towards: business-to-business organizations, not-for-profit organizations, central and local government, financial services organizations, professional services firms, technology organizations, services companies, non-departmental government bodies and non-governmental organizations (NGOs).

Book structure

Chapter 1 is an introduction to the importance of customers and maintains that a crucial tenet of moving to a value proposition model is putting customers at the heart of everything you do. Chapter 2 explains what a value proposition is and what it isn't and how it belongs at many levels in an organization. Chapter 3 explores the value-focused approach and Chapter 4 introduces the Value Proposition Builder™, the main focus of this book and the practical guide to help you build your value proposition. Chapters 5 through to 10 detail the six steps to building your value proposition. Chapter 11 shows two outputs from the building process, the value proposition template and statement. Chapter 12 shows how to create messaging from your value proposition outputs, and Chapter 13 looks at aspects of implementation across the organization. Chapter 14 gives a short guide as to how to get started immediately and how to keep your value proposition alive over time and Chapter 15, the final chapter, takes a look at how you can become a value-focused enterprise.

We sincerely hope that you find the book thought-provoking, practical and useful in helping you focus on building a profitable organization. We have created a webpage for ongoing discussions on this topic and welcome your input to the discussions. Please join the debate at www.valueproposition.biz.

1 What do you *really* think about customers?

Introduction

A midweek morning in the spring of 1989, in an otherwise empty chic London Italian restaurant, four men and a woman, all in their late twenties or early thirties, sit around a table drinking strong coffee from frequently replenished cafetières placed on the crisp white tablecloth. They talk animatedly, good-humoredly, with intensity. The subject? What their company, an advertising agency, stands for. Why, five years previously, they had broken away from other agencies to found it. What has made it successful and what makes it different, special.

Looking on, a man listens intently to the conversation and, every so often, probes to find out more about a particular aspect of the discussion, or shifts the conversation in a new direction. Around the table two cameramen move unobtrusively, capturing the shifting dynamics of the conversation on film. A sound recordist optimizes the sound pickup through carefully positioned microphones.

What's going on here is a result of the advertising agency commissioning a film to showcase some of its work and give prospective clients an insight into the company's philosophy. The head of the film production company – the guy listening and asking questions – recognized that a key part of the advertising agency's offering is its passion for what it does; which is why he proposed this roundtable, free-flowing approach to getting the principals' thoughts and ideas on film. The final output

– a seven-minute, tightly edited, fast-paced film with high production values – will succeed in getting across the energy, the passion, the excitement of their organization.

Now fast forward 20 years to 2009. Our corporate film producer is still in business but the world has changed. In the nascent internet, minimally broadband-enabled world of the late 1980s, corporate video was a must-have part of the marketing mix, backed by good budgets. Twenty years later, technological advances have put video within easy – and easily distributable – reach of many more users. Rather in the way that Microsoft PowerPoint has empowered everyone to become a presentation expert (or so they think!), new video technologies have enabled just about anyone to make videos.

In face of this, our film producer finds life more difficult. The budgets required to make the kinds of films he used to make are hard to come by. Too frequently, prospective clients say: 'How much? You must be joking! We can make a film for a fraction of that!' And, of course, they're right.

So what is our film producer to do? A clue comes from a client testimonial that the film producer has. A senior executive in a global company said: '[His] films have been part of helping transform the way we communicate our marketing objectives internally… The films are not inexpensive but the creative result means our people watch them. [He] delivers great value and I would recommend him unreservedly.'

What is actually happening here, as you may have gathered, is that the most valued thing about our film producer is not that he makes films. The greatest value comes from his ability to facilitate the analysis of situations to get absolute clarity, so that messages can be brilliantly communicated. And, in today's business world, that's a skill worth its weight in gold.

Think about it: this insight brings profound implications for the way our film producer conducts his business. For instance, it implies that his competitors (the clients' alternative sources of supply) are not – or not just – other film production companies. It means, too, that for as long as our film producer continues to lead his business on the basis of its being a 'corporate film production company', prospects will assess it on that basis and may try to drive down prices to a commoditized, lowest common denominator. If all a prospect's procurement experts are worrying about is the relative cost of a cameraman, or a sound recordist, or the hourly rate in an edit suite, they will have completely missed the point… and our chap will have lost the business.

The important factor is the client experience. What issues does the film production company address or solve for a client? Why do those issues occur, and what underpins them? And what other companies (markets, segments, specific companies) experience those issues and would, therefore, represent good sales opportunities?

These are the issues this book sets out to illuminate. We are talking about value propositions. And let's make it clear from the outset that *a value proposition is not what you do. It is the value experience that you deliver.* In the example just given – which is factual but disguised – our film maker's Value Proposition is not that he makes good films!

The films that he makes may be wonderful but the value delivered is something else, and something that is hugely more valuable.

What do you *really* think about customers?

The events most critical to a business happen outside the firm managing it. These are the events that the customer experiences as a result of using and interacting with the firm's products, services, and actions. Yet these resulting experiences and their implications often escape the real attention of managers in conceiving and executing business strategy.

(*Delivering Profitable Value*, Michael J. Lanning,
Perseus Publishing, 1998)

This book is about value propositions (VPs): what they are (and what they are not); their importance in the successful running of a 21st-century business; how to create them; and how to apply them. To be clear, we have used the terms 'client' and 'customer' interchangeably throughout this book.

What is important to understand is that there may well be, of course, more than one customer in the chain. For example, a hardware manufacturer may sell through resellers who, in their turn, sell to end users. Identifying the customer chain is important because value propositions depend on your being able to analyse, quantify and articulate the experience that a customer will receive when choosing your offering.

So, before we get into the value story, it's useful to take a step back to consider attitudes towards clients and their customers. Why? Because the way we think about clients and their customers is a key influencer of the way we think about business in general, and marketing and selling in particular. This is important because value propositions can only function within what we term a value-focused enterprise, and value focus is a function of the way clients and customers are viewed and treated.

So what is your client mindset? Often, our attitudes towards client–supplier relationships are deeply ingrained and go to one or other of two extremes:

- *Inside-out:* 'Clients must be persuaded to buy what our organization decides they should buy, based on ease and convenience for our organization.'
- *Outside-in:* 'Clients must be supplied with whatever goods or services they say they want.'

In today's marketplaces, both of these approaches risks driving a business into bankruptcy. A value-focused approach using VPs is different because it requires you to put yourself in your customer's shoes... and before you can put on someone else's shoes, you have to take off your own.

Both the inside-out and outside-in models are confrontational, based on the fact that one party must win and one must lose: see Figure 1.1. The value-focused model is different: see Figure 1.2.

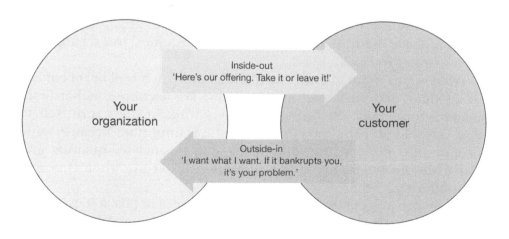

Figure 1.1   The inside-out and outside-in models

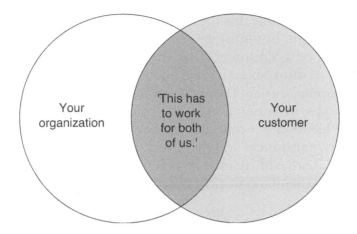

Figure 1.2   The value-focused approach

Before exploring the value-focused approach in more detail, let's explore the fundamental idea of a 'customer'.

The lessons of childhood

Because we have all engaged in transactions from an early age, our attitudes and beliefs about buying and selling are often ingrained to the point of fossilization. When you were a child you probably played at 'shopping', pretending to be either the customer or the storekeeper, handing over pretend money in return for pretend commodities. Then, very early on, that business simulation translated itself seamlessly into reality when you handed over real money in return for real comic books and the other essentials of early life. So, by the time you reached maturity, the business of buying things was second nature, and the notion of being a customer was so innate as to be completely internalized and unconsidered.

That's the problem. It means that when any of us uses the word 'customer' its meaning and implications are taken for granted. We assume that everyone has a shared, common definition of 'customer' – not only in the literal sense of 'an acquirer of a good or service', but also in the underlying behavioural and emotional components that we associate with customer–supplier relationships. So, when terms like 'customer-centric' and 'customer-focused' enter the business lexicon, we automatically assume that there is a shared, common understanding of what they mean. But is there?

The notion of a 'customer' that the majority of people hold (not that many of us think about it very much) is a product of the Industrial Age. As historian Norman Davies has pointed out: 'Once the Industrial Revolution was in motion… In the purely economic sphere, the growth of the money economy turned self-sufficient peasants into wage-earners, consumers and taxpayers, each with new demands and aspirations.'[1] And, with particular reference to the Depression years, the authors of a book on world's fairs have written:

> Progress, in addition to its other definitions, now meant increased consumer spending as world's fair sponsors tried to persuade Americans that they had to set aside older values such as thrift and restraint and become consumers of America's factory and farm products. By rebuilding America's domestic market, so the argument ran, consuming citizens could hasten America's economic recovery and put the United States back on track toward fulfilling its utopian potential.[2]

It is interesting to conjecture the form that recovery from the Depression of 2008/09 may take!

As a result of these influences and more ('Appendix A: Back to the future' provides a brief overview of some of the influences) many of the client–supplier approaches that we now experience are based on implicit or explicit promises and threats. Many enterprises still approach their clients with the aim of winning against them, rather than winning with them. However, the notion of 'client/customer' is a concept and a set of associated behaviours entirely under conscious control and, therefore, capable of re-evaluation and redesign.

The experience of now

The value proposition approach to business strategy and operations is, effectively, the necessary re-evaluation and redesign that recognizes clients and their customers in a new and powerfully productive way. It recognizes that businesses need to generate profits to survive, but that there can be no business and no profit unless the client is recognized as a lead stakeholder with whom you need to form a collaborative but not slavish relationship. In the 21st century, a service or solutions provider that does not recognize this fact will fail.

Are you able to acknowledge the importance of the client? Do you believe it? Do you *really* believe it?

We ask you to confront this issue because a belief in the paramount importance of serving and delivering measurable value to clients is essential to an understanding of client value propositions... but it can be a hard idea to buy in to.

The fact that many people pay lip service to client importance but do not really believe it is surely borne out by the fact that many people equate 'marketing' with-sleight-of hand activity designed to con people into paying good money for more than they actually receive. (There was wild audience applause when the late, polemical stand-up comedian Bill Hicks said: 'By the way, if anyone here is in advertising or marketing, kill yourselves... There's no rationalization for what you do and you are Satan's little helpers. You are the ruiners of all good things.'³) And little wonder that 'sales' is often experienced as a coercive activity designed to 'get one over' on customers. In fact, some companies have now banned the word 'sales' from their organizations, opting for the emotionally neutral term business development.

Why does this situation exist? Well, it's because the entire Western business model in the 19th and 20th centuries was built to benefit, variously, shareholders, politicians, producers, and retailers – rather than customers. That's not to say that customers got nothing out of it, but they were down the line in the value stakes. In fact, at no time since the dawn of the industrial age have customers' needs and interests been a primary focus of business activity... until now.

Customer primacy was bubbling up in the second half of the 20th century, when its most active supporters were not in the United States or Europe, but in Japan. In the late 20th century, Mr Taiichi Ohno, the genius behind the Toyota lean manufacturing system, said: 'All we are doing is looking at the timeline from the moment the customer gives us an order to the point when we collect the cash. And we are reducing that timeline by removing the non-value-added wastes.'⁴ A huge amount of wisdom is packed into those few words. It's what enabled Toyota to achieve customer focus and, in 2007, to become the world's No. 1 automotive manufacturer.

But, if you have been brought up in a Western style consumer society, you may not have thought through the reality or implications of client/customer ascendancy. That is not meant in a critical sense.

It's just that you may well automatically accept the old client/customer proposition that has now passed its sell-by date. Yes, you may understand that information and communications technology has enabled globalization, so that competitors are able to strike from anywhere in the world, and quickly produce me-too offerings. Yes, you may understand that the old sources of industrial strength have evaporated. Yes, you may recognize that new technologies and new competition have handed power to clients/customers, giving them greater choice and the ability to exercise that choice. Yes, you may accept that all of this has altered, and continues to alter, our world in astonishing ways. But the old beat-up-on-the-customer model is so embedded in our cultures and our mental models that mentally and emotionally you still may not have taken on board the absolute outcome of these shifts.

The great management thinker Peter Drucker may have stated that the purpose of any business is to create customers. The great adman David Ogilvy may have warned his people that 'the consumer is not a moron, she is your wife'. But the vested interests and sheer inertia to maintain a 'push' marketing and sales model throughout the 20th century proved irresistible.

It was all too convenient. The old corporate model exhibited many of the characteristics of a feudal society – 'the company as fortress'. Inside the corporate keep, in a rigid hierarchy, the hierarchy ruled and loyalty was expected. Departments often coexisted in a state of 'cooperative aggression': internecine guerrilla warfare and, in the worst instances, outright interdepartmental hostilities sometimes broke out. These behaviors, although boredom-relieving or even entertaining for the participants, negatively impacted an organization's ability to serve its clients and their customers. Vast amounts of energy were expended on non-value-adding internal matters: a focus on vertically isolated hierarchies in which individuals concentrated on personal advancement; a tendency to self-perpetuating, bureaucratic activities unrelated to any real business goals; and a concentration on the convenience of the organization rather than the requirements of its customers.

These behaviors may have worked when there was a general belief in the dominance of market share as a moat protecting large organizations against competitive incursion, and for as long as customers accepted a lowly position in the scheme of things and remained 'grateful' for the

Table 1.1 A summary of key changes, pre-millennium versus post-millennium, for corporate success and prosperity

Pre-millennium	Post-millennium
Success depended on	Success depends on
• Control and exploitation of resources • Secrecy, particularly in financial affairs • Intensity of rivalry with competitors • Keeping the workforce in line • Growing market share • Convincing customers to buy what was on offer (including, sometimes, the use of exaggerated claims, bribery and misdirection)	• Wise use of resources, and conservation • Transparency, particularly in financial affairs • Working with customers to identify and respond to their needs and wants, and responding honestly to those requirements • Speed of innovation and response to customer needs and wants, including the articulation of supportable, measurable *value propositions* • Active engagement of workforce intelligence, creativity and enthusiasm… in marketplaces where talent is increasingly scarce • Coordination and leverage of systems
Prosperity meant competing with	Prosperity means working with
• Customers • Workforce (command and control) • Suppliers • Competitors	• Customers • Workforce (empower and enable) • Suppliers • Competitors (sometimes)

goods and services on offer. But it's different now; such behaviors are absolutely counterproductive (see Table 1.1).

Now, failure to acknowledge that the weight of competition out there will tend to push your organization's offerings down the slide towards commoditization, and that those competitors are able to launch 'me-too' and 'new concept' offerings in astonishingly short time frames, can lead quickly to a fall. The imperative to do things in new ways means that organizations need to achieve new levels of 'fitness' in order to be creative, responsive and flexible. Bureaucratic tendencies (ie self-serving, non-customer-focused activities) will lead to corporate sclerosis and failure.

And we now all have to take account of ethical issues that have arisen as a consequence of industrial activity generally, and of globalization. Concern for and protection of our environment, inclusion and diversity in workforces, and honesty and integrity in global dealings, are just three examples of ethical issues that enterprises need now to embrace.

More and more, organizations make value judgments about their alliance partners and suppliers on the basis of their ethical performance. Companies may completely exclude would-be suppliers or partners from work, based on any failure to uphold certain ethical standards.

Technology and customer power

This is a book about value propositions, but a brief diversion to the technological environment is in order.

Company references in books of this kind are notoriously risky: all too often, examples held up as paragons of some feature or other crash and burn. Nonetheless, it is noteworthy that, at the start of November 2007, Google overtook Procter & Gamble in terms of market capitalization, to become the world's fifth most valuable company. At that time, Google was about ten times as valuable as General Motors. What more potent demonstration of the fact that the Information Age has supplanted the Industrial Age? This is an ongoing motive force behind client/customer power.

Customer access to real-time online information means that it is easy for people to check and validate the specifications, availability and, often, pricing of goods and services from around the world. The old limits have gone. We now live in a frontierless world where product and service providers are able to enter into dialogue with people who, previously, would have been inaccessible to them. Thanks to new technologies, providers are now head to head with customers as at no time since the age of door-to-door selling. If you fail to impress, a search engine will take the prospect swiftly to a competitor who does. And competitors are myriad.

Added to this, disintermediation has driven prices down and led to the blurring of industry boundaries as new products and services come from hitherto unexpected sources – financial services from supermarket operators, for example. It means, too, that through aggregation markets in specialized products and services have become viable and attractive – part of the 'long tail' effect.[5]

It is a very different world from that of the 20th century, and one that is moving ever more quickly in the direction of customer empowerment. Just consider for a moment the ongoing technological trends and drivers:

- the availability of technologies (service-oriented architectures and the like) that do away with the tyranny of siloed legacy systems;
- the accelerating convergence of devices such as the PC, TV and mobile phone;
- the availability of software-as-a-service;
- the socially revolutionary effects of Web 2.0;
- new kinds of device connectivity to give access to new services (such as telematics: why shouldn't a specially tagged undershirt recognize when a patient's heart rate or blood pressure move out of acceptable ranges, and send a signal to the doctor?)

Growing up with all of these technologies, the child of the internet generation has an understanding of the customer's importance to any enterprise. Anyone born earlier has to make the conscious mental adjustment.

Finally, an obvious but crucial point about the technology-enabled Information Age: we are all being bombarded each day with more messages, via more media, than ever before. Because all manner of material is competing for our attention, our auto response is to be more selective. We brutally filter out a great deal of material, based on almost instantaneous judgements about the relevance or otherwise of any particular item. This may be a necessary means to keep ourselves sane, but oh what a challenge it creates for bona fide communication!

This is a major reason for the emergence of the value proposition in business. If you have, metaphorically and sometimes literally, a few seconds to get your target audience to hear you before moving straight on to consider your competitor, you'd better have your value proposition beautifully worked out, honed, and articulated so that it relates directly to that prospect's needs and hot buttons. This was a major driver, particularly in technology markets, in leading people to think that a value proposition is nothing more than just a marketing message.

USP, FAB, VP, POP/POD: analysing the alphabet soup

At a conference where Professor Neil Rackham, internationally acknowledged sales guru, was the keynote speaker he asked delegates to define a value proposition. The first person to reply said: 'It's marketing bullshit for a benefits statement.' This is completely incorrect, but it is probably what most people think. So let's briefly review the techniques that enterprises have used in the recent past to try to express competitive differentiation.

Although the Information Age has now supplanted the Industrial Age, the transition was not totally abrupt. As mentioned earlier, Japanese innovators recognized the need to eliminate non-value-adding activities, and were culturally much more attuned than their Western counterparts to the power of collaboration, as evidenced by their *Kaizen* (continuous improvement) approach.

When, late in the 20th century, the globalization tipping point happened, enabling supply to approach and exceed demand, and when Japanese goods were enthusiastically being snapped up, Western companies at long last recognized the imperative to produce quality goods. But even then, it took a while for many companies to understand that quality has to be built in to products and services, rather than being 'inspected in'.

In the mid- to late 20th century, companies often tried to identify for their products and services a unique selling proposition, or USP. This was, as the term suggests, something that made a product or service 'special', something that could be thrown into a sales situation as a clincher to get the deal. Bizarrely, however, USPs often were not directly related to value and, sometimes, not even directly related to the product or service. In the 1970s, for example, such was the paucity of quality, thinking and innovation in British automotive manufacturing

Table 1.2   The FAB concept

Feature		Advantage		Benefit
This car has a 6 liter engine...	... which means that ...	... it goes fast...	... which means that ...	... you can get to the office more quickly.
This car has a 1 liter engine...	... which means that ...	... it is fuel efficient...	... which means that ...	... it causes less damage to the planet
This firm has 500 consultants ...	... which means that ...	... there are plenty of people to handle your work...	... which means that ...	... you can rely on our availability.
This machine has fewer moving parts...	... which means that ...	... there are fewer things to go wrong...	... which means that ...	... you get less downtime and more productivity.

that a motor car was presented with the USP of a 'square' steering wheel!

Next, 'features and benefits' emerged as an advance on USPs. In fact, the formula evolved to 'features–advantages–benefits', which gave the handy acronym FAB. In countless workshops in the 1970s and 1980s delegates learned that features were connected to advantages, and advantages to benefits, by the linking phrase '... which means that ...' (Table 1.2).

You get the idea? Fab! There was often no great effort to prove the claims, and the idea at the time was to create as long a list as possible. More, so the thinking went, was better.

Then, the truth dawned... *a feature is not a benefit unless it is a solution to a need.* This was perhaps the moment that the concept of the value proposition was born. Even then, it took time to get to today's understanding of the term.

The first post-FAB differentiating technique compared a product or service with its competitor(s) by listing points of parity (POP) and points of difference (POD). This had the virtue of at least acknowledging competitive offerings. POP–POD analyses, however, were not necessarily discriminating in relation to a particular customer's need or situation. The time for the value proposition had arrived.

However, no sooner had value proposition entered the business lexicon than it started to be misapplied. It became used as an alternative for USPs, features, benefits, POPs and PODs. So, for example, people assume that statements like the following are value propositions: 'Our new content management system enables enterprises to store and retrieve all of their data from one source'; 'Our law firm is staffed with highly qualified lawyers'; 'We are able to provide low-cost outsourced services'. But as you will now recognize, these are not value propositions. They are not even benefits: they are features.

Client-focused, not client-run

Having so emphatically made the point that the client and client needs are central to the success of any enterprise, it is important to reinforce the point that client focus does not mean responding slavishly to whatever a client demands, nor just doing what a client asks. The ultimate purpose of an enterprise is to create wealth, so there would be no point in responding to client demands that might result in bankruptcy.

It's more complex than that, however. As Steve Jobs, co-founder of Apple, says: 'You can't just ask customers what they want and then try to give that to them. By the time you get it built, they'll want something new.'

In some circumstances (particularly where new products or services are concerned) clients may not understand whether or not a particular offering will be of value to them. In these situations the value proposition approach is far more powerful than old-style marketing-speak, because it enables a new offering to be expressed in terms of *the value of the client experience that it will deliver.*

That's the heart of this entire concept. Clients do not buy 'things'. They buy the experiences that those 'things' are able to deliver. And, when so doing, they measure the benefits against the costs. Which leads us directly to consider: what is a value proposition?

Notes

1. *Europe, A History*, Norman Davies, Oxford University Press, 1996, page 771.
2. *Fair America – World's Fairs in the United States*, Robert W. Rydell, John E. Findling and Kimberly D. Pelle, Smithsonian Institution Press, 2000, page 11.
3. Bill Hicks on marketing.
4. *Toyota Production System: Beyond large-scale Production*, Taiichi Ohno, Diamond, Inc, 1978; English translation, 1988
5. *The Long Tail*, Chris Anderson, Random House, 2006.

2 What is a value proposition?

Strategy is based on a differentiated customer value proposition. Satisfying customers is the source of sustainable value creation. Strategy requires a clear articulation of targeted customer segments and the value proposition required to please them. Clarity of this value proposition is the single most important dimension of strategy.

(*Strategy Maps*, Robert S. Kaplan and David P. Norton, HBS Press, 2004)

The same comparison is true today of value propositions as was true for quality in its early days in the 1970s and 1980s. Quality had to be built into the products and services sold, rather than being 'inspected in'. Total quality management (TQM) became the process by which quality was built in through the entire organization.

As defined by the International Organization for Standardization (ISO):

TQM is a management approach for an organization, centered on quality, based on the participation of all its members and aiming at long-term success through customer satisfaction, and benefits to all members of the organization and to society.

Whereas TQM managed the discipline of thrift through 'Right First Time' approaches, value proposition development, when operationalized throughout the business, is an organizational approach to building in value to the customer experience – the management of the discipline of providing profitable customer value.

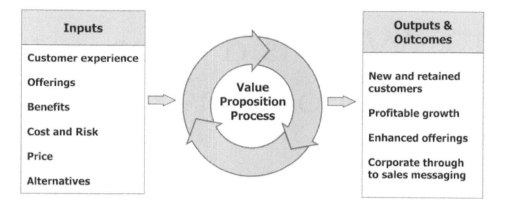

Figure 2.1 The value proposition process (VPP) has inputs and outputs; the classic value proposition statement is only one of the messaging outputs

As with TQM, building a value proposition is a conversion and focusing process. It has inputs, processes and outputs, as can be seen in Figure 2.1.

To distinguish between the value proposition development process and the outputs of this process, we will now refer to the process as the value proposition process (VPP).

We will look at the specific steps involved in building a value proposition later, but it's important to highlight the point again that this is an approach which has inputs, a process and outputs.

One of the outputs of the VPP is a set of messages that can be used for internal and external communication. So a value proposition statement is *a clear, compelling and credible expression of the experience that a customer will receive from a supplier's measurably value-creating offering.* It is not a description of what your organization does for a customer.

Lanning[1] says:

A value proposition is:

● *about* customers but *for* your organization;
● not addressed to customers but must drive these communications;
● articulates the essence of a business, defining exactly what the organization fully intends to make happen in the customer's life.

Value proposition thinking is at the heart of any value-focused organization. It sharpens the way organizations work by focusing activity so as to serve customers profitably. Note the use of 'profitably': the value proposition approach recognizes that you must be profitable to stay in business. A value proposition approach does not mean that your organization responds to every customer or prospect demand. That would be a sure path to bankruptcy.

Why do you need to build a value proposition?

The key to the answer lies in the definition in the first few paragraphs of this chapter – that value proposition development is an organizational approach to building in value to the customer experience; it is the management of the discipline of providing profitable customer value.

It is simply that by building a value proposition you will provide profitable and superior customer value, more profitable and more superior than if you hadn't built one. The whole object is to generate wealth. By providing superior and profitable customer value you are increasing your own wealth.

Alvin Toffler once said: 'Profits, like sausages… are esteemed most by those who know least about what goes into them.' But we know that a key way of building profits is to build value propositions. One of the building blocks of value proposition creation is the customer experience (what we term the value experience in Chapter 6).

Our focus is on business-to-business markets, where more quantitative research still needs to be done, but in consumer markets Forrester's Customer Experience Index shows that a good customer experience is closely aligned with loyalty and a disinclination to switch to a different supplier. Retailers delivering the worst customer experience are losing out an estimated $184 million a year in revenue and for large banks the worst performers can be $242 million behind the industry leaders.

In Chapter 6 we explore further how a focus on customer experience delivers profit.

Some definitions

The problem with the term 'value proposition' is that it is used so loosely, and its meaning is so assumed, that it means nothing. Or, rather, it means all sorts of things to different people. Mostly, however, it is used as a synonym for 'benefits statement' or to describe the offering. But think about it and you'll realize how inappropriate this is, because value cannot be represented by benefits and offerings alone. It must also take account of costs. This means that:

Value = Benefits minus Cost

where cost stands not only for money but also the other exposures and risks that accompany any transaction. So, time, convenience, physical or mental risk, and so on, all have to be weighed in the balance with any benefits.

From this it follows that value is specific to a particular instance, because time, convenience, perceived risks and so on are all factors that vary from organization to organization and from individual to individual. Value, like beauty, is in the eye (or mind) of the beholder.

So, value propositions must apply to specific situations. Value propositions really have weight where they are related to specific market segments, specific offerings used over specific time frames, specific sales opportunities, and to targeted constituencies within those specific sales opportunities.

This means that it is necessary to define the top-level value proposition (VP) for an organization; *and* for a specific market segment; *and* for a particular offering over time; *and* for a specific sales opportunity for that offering within that segment; *and* for individual influencers (eg chief executive officer, chief information officer, finance, marketing, etc) within that opportunity.

This is not as onerous as it first sounds. Starting from the top level and working down through the levels is much easier than starting at the sales level and then attempting to fit the value proposition back up through the organization (Figure 2.2).

Used properly, value propositions are powerful tools for a range of activities, from the strategic to the tactical. Value propositions answer the following questions:

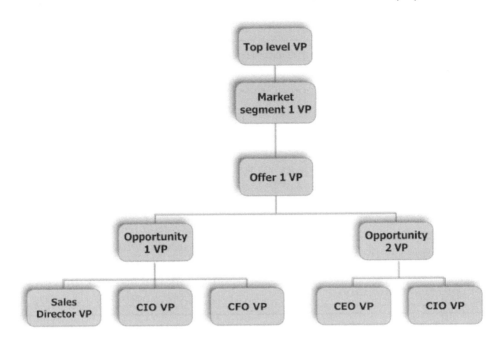

Figure 2.2 When value propositions are developed for each layer, from the top level to the specific influencers within a sales opportunity, they ensure congruence, integrity and precision for messaging and proposals from top to bottom of the organization

- Are we in the right business, focused on the right things for the right clients?
- What is the essence of what we do, with what benefits and at what cost, for whom?
- Are we pursuing the right sales opportunities? (This is increasingly important because, for service and solutions providers, the cost of pursuing opportunities is at an all-time high, and still rising.)
- And, from the opposite (procurement) perspective, are those companies that supply us aligned with our organization and values?

The term 'value proposition' was coined in the 1980s by Michael J. Lanning. He defined it as the essence of a business. A business, he said, is a value delivery system.[2] It must be flattering to Mr Lanning to

Table 2.1 Summary of value proposition outcome

Real and complete value propositions...	
... are not:	... are actionable choices of:
Vague, indecisive platitudes and unactionable lists of general categories	Measurable, specific proposed results
Internally driven statements of what we will do	What will happen for the customer
Customer-compelled regurgitations of what customers say they *want/require*	Experiences that we believe the customer *would value*
Promises of the moon	What we will and will not deliver, and to whom – includes *trade-offs*

Source: Based on DPV Group LLC chart, from information at www.dpvgroup. com.

have seen his coinage become so ubiquitously adopted, but depressing to see it so wrongly used.

Properly understood and applied, a value proposition approach will help you conserve resources by focusing your attention on pursuing viable goals, opportunities and relationships. It will ensure you deal fairly and openly with your clients, meeting their needs in a manner that will also ensure the long-term health of your own business (Table 2.1).

Later, we go into detail about exactly what constitutes client value propositions, and how to develop them, but for now it is important to understand that value propositions are not lists of general benefits, nor corporate positioning statements, nor brand essences, nor general elevator pitches or messages. They are much more specific to the needs and circumstances of prospects and clients.

Our focus in this book is on client value propositions for business-to-business (B2B) situations. Business-to-consumer situations can be different because 'customers in business markets predominantly focus on functionality or performance, whereas customers in consumer markets predominantly focus on aesthetics and taste'.[3]

For a B2B enterprise, selling without value propositions must lead, sooner or later, to value dissipation and commoditization on the basis of that lowest common denominator, price. The ability to identify and articulate client value propositions is therefore not just 'something that marketing and sales do'. It is a differentiating, strategic capability. It relates to the whole organization, starting from the 'C-suite' of top management.

This is of strategic importance because, as outlined in Chapter 1, for the first time since the Industrial Revolution, the customer really is now a primary stakeholder in your business.

Not least, the global financial crisis of 2008/09 has focused minds powerfully on value and integrity. Through the unrestricted use of new but inadequately evaluated financial instruments – particularly securitization – financial services organizations caused pain for their customers to such an extent that it recoiled back on them, putting the entire financial system in jeopardy. Had the value proposition been properly thought through, this need not have happened (Figure 2.3).

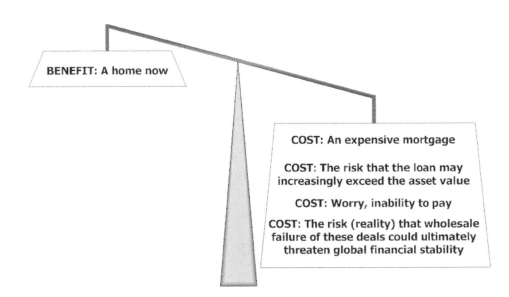

Figure 2.3 It's a no-brainer, with hindsight, admittedly; the trigger underlying the credit crunch and global financial crisis of 2008/09 (aka a very, very, very bad value proposition)

Exploring the value proposition concept

Let's put some flesh on the skeleton of the ideas just presented. If, as already stated, a value proposition statement is *the articulation of the measurable value of the experience that an organization or individual will get from an Offering, where Value = Benefits minus Cost*, it follows that a value proposition must include the following elements:

- Capability – what you can do for a customer.
- Impact – how that will help the customer to succeed.
- Cost – what the customer must pay for the privilege.

The idea of the value proposition follows on from the famously neat point that Harvard marketing professor Theodore Levitt made: 'People don't want to buy a quarter-inch drill. They want a quarter-inch hole.' The company that created and operates the Tesco Clubcard, dunnhumby Associates, has long understood this experience factor. At one stage it printed quirky lines on its stationery. For example: 'People don't buy mobile phones. They buy theatre tickets on buses.' That's the sense of it. It's about the facility or experience delivered, not the details of the product or offering. A value proposition is not about 'us' – our cleverness, our needs, our expectations, the bells and whistles of our offering. Rather it is about the customer's experience of our offering in terms of his or her needs and wants.

Understood and applied properly, a value proposition is a powerful tool to help you determine your capability to succeed. Value propositions work because they force focus. The struggle is important: it's the tool that helps you focus and get the business.

To help clarify value proposition development, in the following chapters we outline a clear process. Before we start on that, however, let's cover a few of the basics…

Value = Benefits minus Cost

OK, we've stated that Value = Benefits minus Cost. Let's just investigate that a little.

In the *Oxford English Dictionary*, 'Value' merits a lengthy set of definitions, including these: 'The amount of a commodity, medium of exchange, etc, considered to be an *equivalent* for something else; a fair or satisfactory *equivalent* or return'; 'The worth, usefulness, or importance of a thing; *relative merit or status* according to the estimated desirability or utility of a thing'; 'The quality of a thing considered *in respect of* its ability to serve a specified purpose or cause an effect' (emphasis added).

You'll have noticed that in every case Value is a relative measure. There's an old English expression: 'One man's meat is another man's poison'. That's the sense of it. The chance of a ticket to the big game (or the safari, or the concert, or whatever) might be a huge motivator for one person, but a complete turn-off for another. Value, like beauty, is in the eye of the beholder.

It follows that expressions of Value cannot be communicated by unidirectional statements. A value proposition must contain both sides of the give-and-take equation: 'This is what offering X will do for you, and here is the cost to you.'

That's why Value = Benefits minus Cost, where 'benefits' and 'cost' are broadly evaluated:

- Benefits are the outcomes and experiences of value to the client (not the features of the offering).
- Cost includes financial exposure *and* other factors (time or risk, for example) that the client must 'pay' to get the benefits.

Take a simple example: automated cash dispensers (ATMs) that enable us to check our bank accounts and withdraw cash. A few decades ago, the only way to draw cash from your account was to write a check for the amount you required, go to a branch of your bank, queue up, and get the bank cashier to swap the check for cash. The problem was that bank opening hours were not customer-friendly, so people had to break away from their work, or whatever else they were doing, to get to the bank. And because a lot of people were only able to get to the bank in their lunch breaks, the queues were long and tiresome... and you ended up hungry.

Then along came the ATM, and it changed the world. So what is the top-level value proposition for an ATM?

The benefits are clear: lots more places to access your cash (normally resulting in fewer or smaller queues), without fuss, whatever time of the day or night. That translates into the ability to get on with your life without this particular disruption or inconvenience.

What about the cost? Well, you may have to pay a direct fee for accessing the money in this way, but cost also comes in the form of risks: the possible risk of fraud though card cloning and the like, and perhaps a slightly higher risk of mugging than exists when you are inside a bank branch.

For most of us, the risks associated with ATM use are more than offset by the convenience we gain, so the top level value proposition is benefit-positive.

However, there are those for whom the ATM value proposition will not stack up: those of a nervous disposition, for example, fearful that their debit card details might be stolen, or their cash snatched; and perhaps those who enjoy the personal contact with a human bank cashier.

OK, this is a simple example, but it serves to make an important point: because value propositions express experiences, they must relate to specific target groups. It is all very well, and necessary, to develop overarching, top-level value propositions, but that is only the start. Thereafter, the challenge is to define value propositions for different people within a target segment and, even, a target company. This point is explained in the BRAIN box later on in this chapter.

To help you get clarity and differentiation by developing value propositions, there follows the Value Proposition Builder™ process. The process is not just theoretical. It has been applied and proven by application to many real client situations, including a specialist offering within a major accounting firm, a global outsourcing organization, and a leading company supplying technological solutions. It works.

Introducing the Value Proposition Builder™

The Value Proposition Builder™, explained in detail in the pages of this book, is a six-step iterative process.

1. First, you need to decide who to talk to. This means analysing and identifying the *market* segments, or specific clients, or target individuals within those clients for whom your solution has the potential to deliver value, profitably.
2. Next, analyse and define the *value experience* that clients get from your organization from its current activities. You need to define

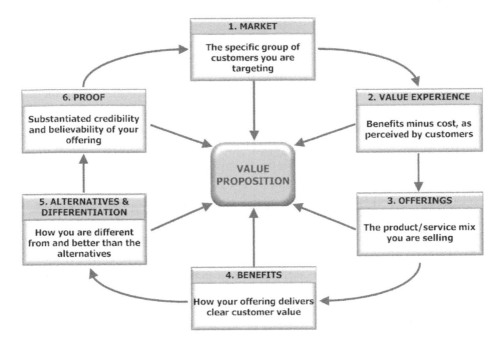

Figure 2.4 The Value Proposition Builder™

good, bad and neutral experiences, but what will really make a difference are those experiential outcomes that have the power of 'Wow!'

3. Then, define the *offerings* mix capable of leveraging your proven value experience with the defined target market group.

4. When you have done this, you are in a position to assess the *benefits* of the offerings in the context of the value experience you are able to deliver to the market group. There is a cost component of benefits here which includes price and customer risks,[4] enabling the calculation of value where Value = Benefits minus Cost.

5. You are then able to go on to work out how that provides *alternatives and differentiation* for your organization...

6. ... and back it all up with relevant, substantiated *proof*.

Crucially, each element is viewed *through the filter of responses already generated*. So, for example, the value experience for a particular situation will be related to specific market segment(s) or client(s) identified in a market. Then, the offering is analysed in terms of the identified value experience related to the specific market segment. And so on. By so doing, you are forced to focus and drill down in ever more specific terms (Figure 2.4).

Value, remember, is in the eye of the beholder, so the focus and drill-down is crucially important. In fact, the more you practise value proposition building, the more you will come to realize that *the real power of value proposition thinking is in the process.* You will come to realize, too, that building value propositions is not easy. It requires hard intellectual analysis and application. Value propositions achieve their compelling power by being complete, credible, costed analyses of the value in given situations.

Professor Neil Rackham likens the situation to mission development sessions. You know the kind of thing: a bunch of senior people lock themselves away for days, weeks, months to hammer out a mission statement. When they emerge, they pin a piece of paper on the notice board. On it is written the sentence that is the result of their thinking. Everyone else gathers round, and there is one overwhelming response: 'It took three months to write *that!*' The point these critics miss is that what was important was the process. So it is with value propositions.

In fact, clients with whom we have facilitated the value proposition building process have talked about it as 'very hard work', 'emotionally intense', 'one of the hardest things we've ever had to do'.

Steps 1, 2 and 3 represent the 'deconstruct' part of the cycle – the process of breaking down and analysing the background to and structure of an offering.

Steps 4, 5 and 6 represent the 'reconstruct' part of the cycle – with the benefit of a complete understanding of the elements of market, experienced value and offering, you are able to build up your value proposition with well-founded, relevant and compelling benefits, alternatives and differentiation, and proof.

Because benefits, alternatives and differentiation, and proof must relate to a specific segment or client situation, it is not possible to construct them until you have analysed market, value experience and offerings.

Note, too, that message development (a term so often confused with value proposition building) happens at Steps 4, 5 and 6. Any 'messages' created earlier in the process cannot be assured of resonance with the market segment or client, the value experience as perceived by a client, and a specific offering.

Focus

The entire value proposition building process is about focus. Going into organizations and asking them what they think their value is, it is our experience that executives adopt a 'more is better' approach. They'll say things like 'We deliver great service', and 'Our intellectual property is really robust', and 'We've got the best people', and so on, and on and on and on. The point is that although these may be interesting features, *they are not differentiating*, and will not make the organization stand out from the crowd.

Put simply, lists of features of this kind provide no directional clarity as to why a particular organization is special. In fact, more usually they get in the way, cluttering the view, so that it becomes impossible for a would-be client to see where the real value is in a given circumstance.

So, much of the purpose of the market, value experience and offerings steps is to strip away features that are irrelevant, unnecessary, and confusing – because they actually detract from a company's value delivery potential.

This stripping away of irrelevancies, and simply too much clutter, to achieve sharp focus can bring uncomfortable emotions to the fore. People don't do this kind of analysis very often and, when they do they find themselves confronting some long- and deeply-held beliefs that may be past their sell-by date, but are seriously hard to let go. However, in a globalized world where continuous change is a key certainty, organizations that avoid this exercise risk finding themselves being powerfully outcompeted.

From top level to specific

Value propositions need to be worked out for all levels of activity, from the top level to the specific. Here's a hypothetical example of the way it works.

BRAIN!

A software developer has developed a new content management system that 'brings' information to online corporate users based on its recognition of the context of their work. That is, it intelligently recognizes the context of their actions and brings only relevant information, saving them a lot of the time and frustration of searching, searching, searching through corporate databanks and external sources for the right material. It's called BRight Access to Information and kNow-how, which gives the convenient acronym BRAIN.

It's very clever. It saves users huge amounts of information search time, and intelligently brings them knowledge, materials and connections that are contextually relevant. The developer is positively aching to tell anyone who will listen all about the smart technical innovations that make BRAIN so good. That's what developers always want to do! He (this kind of developer is always a he ☺) will tell anyone who will listen that BRAIN uses a revolutionary platform, service-oriented architecture and the most advanced taxonomic system in the world. And he will go into loving detail about each element, each of those aspects, each technical widget.

Now, of course, the technical stuff is important, but only in the right context. To the chief executive officer (CEO) of a prospect company it is not only incomprehensible, it is also infuriatingly irrelevant because it does not position BRAIN within the context of the business needs of the company.

So what the software developer needs to do is work out a series of value propositions, along the following lines (Figure 2.5).

Top level

At the top level the value proposition can only be constructed around broad facts that have a relevance to all constituencies. So, for example, the software developer might assemble general facts, including: 40 per cent of an office worker's time is spent trying to manage or repurpose documents. (This is a genuine statistic reported by Gartner in 2005[5].)

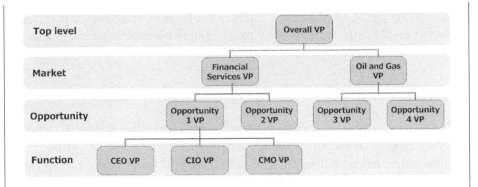

Figure 2.5 Value proposition hierarchy

If BRAIN can be shown to reduce this waste of time, our software developer has the beginnings of a genuine value proposition component. For example, if we assume that the average cost of an office worker is $20,000 per annum, as much as $8,000 of that total may be wasted on this activity alone! If we are able to prove that BRAIN can cut this waste in half, there is a possible saving of $4,000 per office worker.

It is now possible to say that if BRAIN costs $1 million to install, there is a one-year cost break-even in an organization with just 250 office workers. This is an impressive pay-off but, nonetheless, it is just one strand of this particular value proposition, and it is a very general claim. More power can be achieved by drilling down further.

Market

Let's suppose that, as a result of his market analysis and definition work (see Chapter 5) our software developer identifies global financial services players as a key target market for BRAIN. Globalized banking services for the corporate sector involve a large number of high-value sales pitches, involving a lot of information analysis and sourcing, carried out by a lot of employees. Therefore, for the sake of this exercise, we can argue that the pay-off is even better than in the top-level situation.

So, in this sector, let's say that a one-year pay-off for a $1 million investment happens with just 175 office workers. Already, therefore, just in this one aspect, there is a specific difference between the top-level and the market segment value propositions. But our software developer can, and must, do better yet.

Opportunity

Next we come to the opportunity level. Here our software developer needs to devise a value proposition for each opportunity. The value proposition for Global Bank will be specific to Global Bank and, therefore, different from that for its competitor World Bank, and so on.

At the opportunity level, the value proposition for Global Bank will relate directly. For example, if we discover that Global Bank has around 1,000 people in roles that can be positively influenced by BRAIN, then we are able to make a compelling claim about the payback period. The more the value proposition relates to Global Bank's specific circumstances and needs, and the better it describes the positive experience to be gained by acquiring and using BRAIN, the more differentiated and compelling the proposition can be.

But it doesn't end there. Ultimately, value propositions need to be created that are specific to the key influencers and stakeholders within the opportunity.

Function

At the function level, the value propositions will relate to the specific areas of interest and concern of the various stakeholders. For this exercise, let's suppose that, after a couple of decades of focus on process streamlining and cost cutting within Global Bank, to the point where there is no fat left to cut, revenue generation has come to the top of the CEO's agenda. If the CEO-focused value proposition shows that BRAIN can streamline sales processes to accelerate positive sales outcomes, our software developer should get his attention and, we hope, his buy-in.

Likewise, the chief sales officer (CSO) and chief marketing officer (CMO) have a strongly vested self-interest in anything that will make their revenue-generating lives more efficient. For them, however, the value proposition can be couched in more specific sales and marketing terms.

With them – and with the human resources (HR) director, perhaps – the software developer might work out, too, how much BRAIN might help reduce workforce churn by relieving good people of a particularly frustrating chore. If this cuts recruitment and training costs, there is yet another valuable strand to the value proposition.

Meanwhile, the chief information officer (CIO) will likely have a different agenda. For him or her, the value proposition (VP) needs to relate to such issues as systems suitability and compatibility, and ongoing maintenance and cost issues. So, yes, the software developer may have a legitimate reason to talk with the CIO about his or her great technological innovations – but they are of little or no interest, per se, to the other stakeholders.

- Lead: a lead is a clustered selection of information about a prospect or customer: facts, actions and interactions indicating a buying interest.[6]
- Opportunity: a lead where an owner, a budget, a timeline and status are in place.

The VP is a powerful opportunity qualification tool – hugely valuable at times like these, when the costs of pursuing opportunities are very high, and the economic climate is tough. For more on how the value proposition is used as a qualification tool, see Chapter 13.

To sum it up...

A value proposition statement is a clear, compelling and credible expression of the experience that a customer will receive from a supplier's measurably value-creating offering, where Value = Benefits minus Cost. It is not a description of what your organization does for a customer.

The broad components of a VP are:

- Capability: what you can do for a customer.
- Impact: how that will help the customer to succeed.
- Cost: what the customer must pay for the privilege.

A value proposition is a tool that can tell you if you are likely to succeed:

- A value proposition must be compelling and believable.
- Value proposition development needs to be carried out at the top level, market, opportunity and functional levels.
- VPs work because they force focus. The struggle is important: it's the tool that helps you focus your own business and more reliably win business in any sales situation.
- That's particularly important in tough economic times because you need to be sure that whatever resources you commit to sales have the best possible chance of winning.

Notes

1. *Delivering Profitable Value,* Michael J. Lanning, Perseus Publishing, 1998.
2. *Delivering Profitable Value,* Michael J. Lanning, Perseus Publishing, 1998.
3. *Business Market Management – Understanding, creating and delivering value,* James C. Anderson and James A. Narus, Pearson Education International, 2004.
4. As in any business activity, risk is present at every stage, but it is important to differentiate between operational risk (that is, risk relating to your organization) and customer risk (the risk or risks that a customer may experience).
5. Gartner, as reported by *Baseline,* June 24, 2005.
6. The distinction between a lead and an opportunity in the box is referenced from Claus-Peter Unterberger of Oracle, quoted by Neil Rackham.

3 The value-focused approach

A man who knows the price of everything and the value of nothing.

(Oscar Wilde's definition of a cynic)

Value propositions are the essence of a value-focused business approach, which is the only sustainable means to pursue profitability and competitive edge in today's hypercompetitive marketplaces where the cost of pursuing opportunities is at a historical high and still rising.

But what is a value-focused approach, and how is it best to organize a value-focused organization? Getting at the answers requires you to address some fundamentals of your business. Some of the key issues are set out in this chapter:

- What is the difference between a 'traditional' enterprise and a value-focused enterprise?
- With what kind(s) of units of sale is your organization involved? Components? Offers? Solutions? Co-created value?
- What does this mean in terms of the selling approach or approaches being used, or that should be used? Transactional or consultative?
- What is the key strategic value driver in your organization? Product leadership? Operational excellence? Customer intimacy?

The value-focused enterprise[1]

A value-focused enterprise is different from a traditional enterprise. For a long period, the vast majority of businesses operated an inside-out orientation. Latterly, some adopted an outside-in orientation. (The inside-out and outside-in models are overviewed in Chapter 1.) Neither of these is a value-focused enterprise (VFE).

The fact is, resolving to create a VFE requires a fundamental rethink of the way things are organized and managed. This takes us right to the heart of your business strategy and implementation. However large or small your business, from major corporation right down to one-person entity, the underlying business framework can be viewed as shown in Figure 3.1.

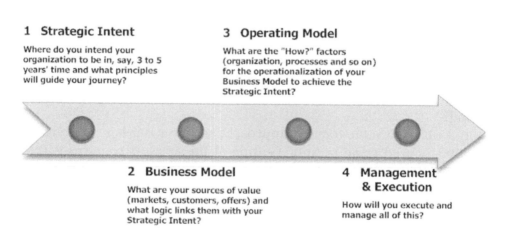

1 Strategic Intent

Where do you intend your organization to be in, say, 3 to 5 years' time and what principles will guide your journey?

3 Operating Model

What are the "How?" factors (organization, processes and so on) for the operationalization of your Business Model to achieve the Strategic Intent?

2 Business Model

What are your sources of value (markets, customers, offers) and what logic links them with your Strategic Intent?

4 Management & Execution

How will you execute and manage all of this?

Figure 3.1 Traditional business framework

This is the traditional way that enterprises plan themselves, whether or not the process is viewed in exactly this way. Often, particularly in smaller companies, the process, in total or in part, is implicit rather than explicit.

In a VFE, the value inputs must start with the strategic intent and be carried all the way through the enterprise. Specifically, *the value proposition becomes the heart of the business model.* Viewed like this, it becomes clear that value propositions are not just something that

1 *Value-centered*
   Strategic Intent

Where do you intend your
organization to be in, say, 3 to 5
years' time, what principles will
guide your journey, and *what is
the Strategic Value Pathway?*

3 *Value-focused*
   Operating Model

What are the "How?" factors
(organization, processes and so on)
for the *operationalization of your
VALUE PROPOSITION* to achieve
the Strategic Intent?

2 *VALUE PROPOSITION*

*What is your VALUE
PROPOSITION (Market, Value
experience, Offerings, Benefits,
Alternatives & Differentiation and
Proof) and how is it congruent
with your Strategic Intent?*

4 *Value-creation-based*
   Management &
   Execution

How will you execute and manage
all of this *to ensure maximum
Value Delivery?*

Figure 3.2 The VFE framework

marketing or sales departments dream up! Value propositions (VPs)
are the basis of the business. They are strategic. They are of crucial
importance to everyone in an organization, starting with the chief
executive officer (CEO) (Figure 3.2).

This is not just a matter of replacing 'business model' with 'value
proposition': it is a fundamentally different way of thinking about,
organizing and running a business. Using this model, you are able to
plan your business (or organization of whatever kind) on the basis of
value to be delivered. In this book we focus very much on the value
proposition phase and not the whole supply chain restructuring or
operationalizing within the business that may be necessary to fully turn
your organization into a value-focused enterprise. However, we have
included some basics about value-focused enterprises in Chapter 15.

When you adopt value-focused thinking at the strategic and business
model levels (that is, the top VP level, as outlined earlier) and pursue
VP analysis and refinement right through to the individual people in
sales opportunities, you are assured of an alignment between the top
management in the 'C-suite' and the company's marketing and sales
people, and everyone in between. Just as total quality management was
at the core of a manufacturing organization's business model, so value
must be at the core of a value-focused enterprise's business model.

Value creation, alignment and decision making

Because decision making can create or destroy value, it is a very important issue. Organizations make countless decisions on a continuous basis, from the solution of simple operational problems to the resolution of complex issues involving trade-offs between multiple and sometimes conflicting objectives. It is the cumulative effect of these decisions that governs value creation or destruction, and, ultimately, corporate performance.

For business-to-business (B2B) companies, there is the need for a level of dynamic client responsiveness that, if it is to be achieved without suboptimizing performance, needs to be based on an alignment of thinking throughout an organization. After all, dynamic customer responsiveness carries with it the risk of suboptimizing performance.

Enlightened organizations recognize that *better decisions do not come from greater control, but from better coordination.* These enterprises accept that they cannot tell employees what to do in all circumstances. Conditions change too fast for that. Decision making needs to be based on clear guidelines – as provided by value proposition thinking.

The Amazon Experience: a strategy based on customer experience

Jeff Bezos, founder and CEO of Amazon, says the strategy for Amazon is threefold with respect to finding the elements that matter to customers, that are durable in time, and where they can build flywheels that they can continue to put energy into.

The three big flywheels are selection, price and availability. He says: 'So if you look at each of those, we know that 10 years from now, customers will still care about selection. We know they will still care about availability and price. They'll want to get their products quickly. So the energy that we put into building those flywheels today will continue to pay dividends, even ten years from now.'

Here is Amazon senior vice-president (SVP) Sebastian Gunningham's[2] overview of Amazon's growth model. While not intentional, it does fit nicely with Amazon's recent earnings announcement of another great quarter.

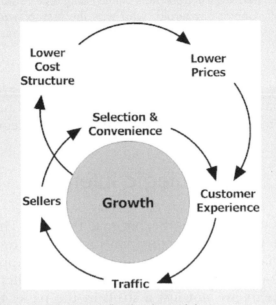

Figure 3.3 The Amazon 'flywheel' model

Sellers drive selection and convenience, which is a key component for a great customer experience (most importantly one-click checkout, A–Z guarantee and its straightforward, consistent merchandising). We highlight here Amazon's expansion to more categories internationally, the well-publicized 3P seller growth and the new product ads programme.

This selection and Amazon's leading online shopping experience generate traffic (78 million-plus registered, global users in 2007 who have purchased once in the last 12 months from an Amazon site) with a heavy sprinkle of repeat buyers who keep coming back for the convenience (I know I do).

The growth in transactions and sales drives scalability and a lower cost structure, which in turn Amazon passes on to consumers in the form of lower prices.

While the model and its concepts are not revolutionary, it helps to understand how Amazon looks at online retailing dynamics and customer satisfaction, and ultimately gains more share of the online shopping world.

Many analysts look at the difference between eBay and Amazon. Where eBay has limited control over transactions on its site as ultimately its marketplace is built on trust, Amazon took a different and more costly approach. It built its own warehouses and a massive distribution network. As a result Amazon can guarantee delivery. For buyers, that can make a big difference.

'Amazon is a retailer; it understands online commerce', said Derek Brown, an analyst with Cantor Fitzgerald, who was the first to warn investors of eBay's weakness. 'They own the experience from start to finish.'

A fuller explanation of the VFE model is provided in Chapter 15. Right now, however, let's take a look at the start point, strategic intent.

Strategic intent

Setting your strategic intent is the 'big goal' thinking. This is where you describe where you want your organization to be in two to five years' time and, crucially, the guiding principles that will apply throughout the journey. Your strategic intent needs to be challenging (so that the next few years are not just a stroll in the park) but achievable (because impossible goals quickly become dispiriting and are, frankly, pointless).

A key value issue here has to do with the fact that, in today's economic climate, and with the vast amount of actual and potential competition that all businesses face, it is not possible to be all things to all people. This is a theme that you'll find we keep coming back to: so, for example, in Chapter 5, 'Market', we talk about going 'narrow and deep' into market niches rather than going 'wide and shallow' in the mistaken – and costly! – belief that it will increase the odds of success.

Sharp focus is the goal, and it's something that starts early in the process, at the strategic intent phase. To help, some great thinking is available from the work of Messrs. Treacy and Wiersema,[3] who have defined a set of three strategic value pathways. They are:

- Operational excellence – delivering value by achieving continuous low cost for customers, as, for example, Wal-Mart. (Icon: Henry Ford.)
- Product leadership – delivering value through product innovation and excellence, as, for example, Harley Davidson, Nike, Swatch, Apple. (Icon: Thomas Edison.)

- Customer intimacy – delivering value by understanding that a client has underlying challenges that can only be met by 'solutions', as, for example, any professional services firm and most of the IT services sector. (Icon: Thomas Watson of IBM fame.)

Treacy and Wiersema persuasively show that a company is only able to put one of these three pathways at the top of its agenda because the emphases of each are on different goals, processes and organizational structures. For example, a product leadership company needs to have the organizational flexibility within which innovators feel empowered and comfortable; but that sort of organization would be inappropriate for an operational excellence focus, where standardization is the way to win. So, a company must choose its primary strategic value pathway and, by so doing, consciously relegate the other pathways to second place (Table 3.1).

Can the same company operate different strategic value pathways?

As just stated, Treacy & Wiersema argue that an enterprise must opt for one of the three strategic value pathways, and relegate the others. But situations may not always be that straightforward.

Take, for example, an information technology (IT) services enterprise that offers database capacity and a selection of applications – customer relationship management (CRM) and so on. Selling server storage capacity does not often depend on any great differentiation of product or service from client to client. It is often a commoditized offering where buyers know what they want and are able to shop around. A buyer's concern is: 'What's your best price per petabyte?' (although there are always ways to differentiate with alternatives as we will see with a storage example used in a 'total cost of ownership' model in Chapter 10).

Selling a CRM application to a major business is quite different. The client company will likely be looking for a tailored application – one that takes account of the client's particular circumstances, customers, and organization

Efficiently selling database capacity requires a brilliant 'engine' that will perform repeatedly, reliably and cost-effectively to enable prospects to acquire capacity easily. In other words, an operational

Table 3.1   Drive better value every year

	Operational excellence	Product leadership	Customer Intimacy
Strategic value pathway*	• Best total cost	• Best product	• Best total solution
Golden rule	• Variety kills efficiency	• Cannibalizing your success with breakthroughs	• Solve the client's broader problem
Core processes	• End-to-end product delivery	• Invention • Commercialization • Market exploitation	• Client acquisition & development • Solution development
Improvement levers	• Process redesign • Continuous improvement	• Product technology • R&D cycle time	• Problem expertise • Service customization
Major improvement challenges	• Shift to new asset base	• Jump to new technology	• Total change in solution paradigm

*Note: Treacy and Wiersema label the first row of this table, 'Value proposition'. Here, we have relabelled it 'Strategic value pathway' because, in our thesis, it gives direction for the value proposition rather than actually being it.
Source: Modified from *The Disciplines of Market Leaders*, Michael Treacy and Fred Wiersema, Perseus Publishing, 1995.

excellence strategic value pathway. However, the collaborative analysis and development work demanded in a CRM application sale point to a customer intimacy strategic value pathway.

So, yes, the same company may need to operate different strategic value pathways... but this can only be achieved when the different business strands are treated as separate business units. This requirement is further highlighted if we look at value delivery in a different, but intimately connected, way – in terms of the type of sales transactions involved.

The Value Pyramid™

Value comes in a myriad of guises – products and services of every conceivable kind: everything from a bottle of cola or a packet of detergent to an aeroplane or a power station; and from accountancy and legal services, to hairdressing and fine art. Given that we are dealing with a virtually infinite list of things for sale, is there any way to classify them into types, to indicate the nature of the value on offer? Well, yes, they can be classified in terms of the types of transactions, the types of unit of sale, that they represent, as shown in Figure 3.4.

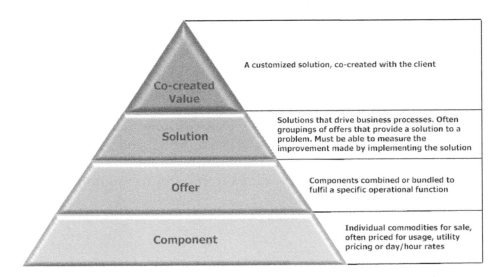

Figure 3.4 The Value Pyramid™: showing units of sale

Let us examine each layer of the Value Pyramid™:

Component

A component is a discrete unit of something capable of being presented and sold on a stand-alone basis. This is obviously a huge category that includes anything and everything from a tin of baked beans or a bottle of cola, to printing a specified number of leaflets on a particular type of paper, to software packages (this document is being drafted using the component Microsoft Word), hardware, consultancy time by the day or legal services by the hour, training companies, and so on and on.

Offer

An offer is a set of components, combined or bundled to fulfil a specific operational function. The Microsoft Word program being used to draft this file came bundled with several other programs as part of the offer, Microsoft Office.

Notice something: components and offers are not majorly differentiated; they are simply 'put out there' in the marketplace for customers to self-select on the basis of recognized needs.

Solution

A solution is a grouping of offers or skills that, as a combined set, deliver a strategic response to a client need. Importantly, the solution is a solution – rather than an offer – because it is recognized as such by the purchaser, and delivers a measurable outcome. As one writer has put it, a solution is 'a mutually shared answer to a recognized problem, and the answer provides measurable improvement'.[4] Moving up the hierarchy of transactions, the change from offer to solution is a step change.

Co-created value

If the shift from offer to solution is a step change, the shift up to co-created value is a giant leap. This is where a provider co-creates a customized solution with a client. The output is a unique, tailored, measurable response to an identified need.

Self-evidently, there are huge differences between selling components and selling co-created value, and it is vital to know the difference. Failure to do so must inevitably result in suboptimal performance and potentially catastrophic failure.

Selling components is a transactional activity where buyers know what they want. Selling co-created value is a consultative activity where buyers know the problem that they want to solve, but don't necessarily know how to achieve it, and, therefore, want to enlist the help of the seller to co-create the solution. Offers and general solutions are on the scale between transactional and consultative. In transactional sales, the role of sales is to *communicate value*, whereas in the consultative sale the role is to *create value*.

An example: for a freelance user or small company, the purchase of Microsoft Word (a component) or Microsoft Office (an offer) is a transactional deal. The buyers are expert in the sense that they know that they require a tool to do a specific task – word processing for creating documents, spreadsheets to manage the accounts, and so on. What they need the supplier to do is communicate the value of the product. Why is this spreadsheet program good? Why is it better than the alternatives? The value is in the product. Period.

By contrast, the buyer of a customer relationship management application for a larger business will likely know what he or she wants to achieve, but may not know how best to achieve it (ie the buyer is an expert influencer but not an expert buyer and the problem is complex). Here, the buyer will want to sit with the provider's experts to co-create the solution. The value is not only in the product or service itself; rather, it is in the consultative dialog that leads to the solution. The sales role, therefore, is to create value.

Transactional and consultative selling

The key differences between transactional and consultative selling are shown in Figure 3.5 and Table 3.2.

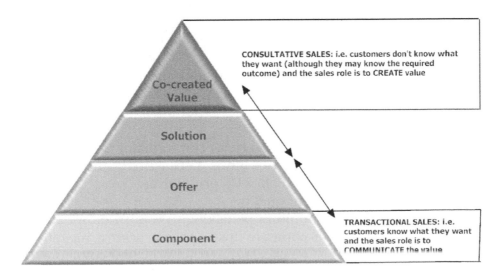

Figure 3.5 The Value Pyramid™: showing the transactional versus consultative sales axis

Table 3.2 Buyer behaviour and motivation in transactional and consultative sales

Type	Buyer behaviour	Motivation
Transactional	Intrinsic value buyers: 'Keep it cheap and easy to do business'	Understands the product Perceives it as substitutable Cost focus Resents time 'wasted' with salespeople
Consultative	Extrinsic value buyers: 'I don't know the answer: help me analyse and solve the issue.'	Focus on how the product is used Interested in solutions and applications Values advice and help Needs the sales person

Source: Modified from *Rethinking the Sales Force: Redefining selling to create and capture customer value,* Neil Rackham and John De Vincentis, McGraw-Hill, 1999.

It is crucially important to identify the mode – transactional or consultative – that is applicable in any particular circumstance. The following story illustrates the point. Replica Co produces a lot of printed materials for prospects, customers, employees, and shareholders. To optimize its print performance and cost, it has created a print-buying capability. Here, Replica Co print buyers compile detailed specifications for items required and invite print companies to pitch for the work. These print buyers are real experts: they know everything there is to know about printing methods, paper stocks, inking, finishing and so on.

So there is really very little leeway for a print company to differentiate itself when talking to this kind of buyer. Let's eavesdrop on a dialog between a print rep and an Replica Co print buyer:

'We deliver excellent print quality.'

'Good. But, frankly, I wouldn't be talking to you if I didn't already know that. We need 1,000 copies of this 16-page brochure, on 130 gsm ivory stock, with a 200 gsm cover, printed litho in four-color process throughout, stitched with two wires. What's your best price?'

'And we have a very strong reputation for meeting print delivery deadlines.'

'Guess what, our other print suppliers all deliver excellent print quality and meet deadlines. I need these brochures delivered here three weeks today. What's your best price?'

'Our clients tell us that we provide great service.'

'Good for them and good for you. Did I mention that four of our other print suppliers are queuing up outside my office door, right now? What's your best price?'

You get the idea. Many companies have realized that, for transactional sales, there may not be a need for a sales force at all. Communicating the value of the service on offer may well be better done via other channels – for example, mail or online. Once the basics are covered, a web-based ordering system may do the job better and certainly cheaper.

But if the requirement was for a non-standard solution, or for some creative thought around the possibilities of printed items, the conversation would be quite different. In fact, the print rep might more likely be talking with a marketing or agency creative person – that is, an expert influencer seeking advice – rather than the transactionally obsessed expert print buyer.

The point is sometimes made that Wal-Mart is one of the world's most focused transactional organizations, but what happens when this doyen of the transactional sale goes hunting for an advertising agency? You guessed it. It switches to consultative mode, because it needs to engage prospective supply partners in analysing the situation and formulating solutions.

Creating value in the consultative sale

New product sales often fail, even where the products are good value. Stranger still, sales often pick up once attention is withdrawn. Why? When Xerox experienced this effect, when launching new colour printing equipment, it set out to find the reason. The following emerged.

A great new product captures the imagination and excitement of the product developers and marketers. So, the marketing department creates materials that communicate the new product features – lovingly listing and explaining all the bells and whistles.

The sales force, presented with these materials, and infused with the general excitement exhibited by their product development and marketing colleagues, go out and show their prospects the product, and all the features it possesses.

The prospect, far from being similarly enthused, gets irritated, thinking: 'What about my needs?'

Armed with this understanding, Xerox tried something different. Its sales people were told not to show pictures of the product, and not to reel off a list of its virtues. Rather, they were instructed to engage their prospects in conversations about the general topic that the product served to satisfy, and to elicit end-user needs. Only then were they permitted to talk specifically about the product, carefully positioning the features and benefits as responses to specifically stated prospect needs.

B2B service and solutions providers and the consultative selling imperative

To remind you, our main focus in this book is on B2B enterprises involved in the provision of services, or service–product amalgams. Sales may happen on a one-on-one, direct supplier-to-client basis, but in many cases will involve such instruments as pre-qualification questionnaires (PQQ), requests for proposals (RFP) and invitations to tender (ITT).

Clients, particularly expert buyers rather than end-user influencers, will often try to make the sales process transactional: 'Here's what we want. What's your best price?' Through adopting a consultative approach and having your value proposition developed, you can often demonstrate to these types of buyers how a VP-based consultative sale has the potential to deliver significantly higher value in terms of quality of deliverables, quality of relationships and quality of the resulting experiences. Sometimes, however, you can't, and this may be a decision point for you to qualify-out of the sale.

It is important to understand this point because the buying cycle in a consultative sale is different from that in a transactional sale. The

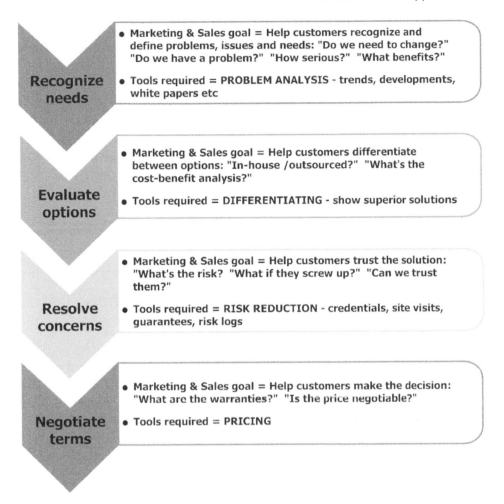

Recognize needs
- Marketing & Sales goal = Help customers recognize and define problems, issues and needs: "Do we need to change?" "Do we have a problem?" "How serious?" "What benefits?"
- Tools required = PROBLEM ANALYSIS - trends, developments, white papers etc

Evaluate options
- Marketing & Sales goal = Help customers differentiate between options: "In-house /outsourced?" "What's the cost-benefit analysis?"
- Tools required = DIFFERENTIATING - show superior solutions

Resolve concerns
- Marketing & Sales goal = Help customers trust the solution: "What's the risk? "What if they screw up?" "Can we trust them?"
- Tools required = RISK REDUCTION - credentials, site visits, guarantees, risk logs

Negotiate terms
- Marketing & Sales goal = Help customers make the decision: "What are the warranties?" "Is the price negotiable?"
- Tools required = PRICING

Figure 3.6 The buying cycle – the form of value creation at each phase of the consultative sales process

Source: Based on Rackham and De Vincentis

buying cycle sequence is shown in Figure 3.6, which shows the process that is emerging as the most successful in consultative sales. A full rationale and description is available in *Rethinking the Sales Force.*[5]

There is more about this crucial aspect of applying value propositions to sales situations in Chapter 13 of this book. For now, keep in mind a point made by Neil Rackham, proven through recent research:

'Extrinsic value customers frequently reject possible suppliers – even those who have good offerings that are attractively priced – if the suppliers push their products or solutions too quickly without first becoming educated in the customer's business.'

The lesson of all this is that value proposition thinking, properly applied, runs from the top to the bottom of an organization. Far from having to do with benefits statements or offerings dreamed up by slick marketers or salespeople, value proposition thinking is at the heart of the strategy and tactics of an enterprise, progressively focused for particular segments, offerings, sales opportunities and, ultimately, individual people within those sales opportunities.

Capgemini – differentiating on the 'how', not the 'what', of deal making

As one of the world's leading consulting, technology and outsourcing providers, Capgemini has a vast amount of experience in framing and selling large, often complicated, deals. The secret of its success, explains Capgemini's vice-president head of outsourcing sales, Bob Scott, owes as much to how it sells as to what it sells.

'Often,' says Bob Scott, 'clients start off thinking that what they want is clear-cut and non-negotiable. They create a request for proposal and tell candidate suppliers to fill in their responses to the list of needs.

'You can see why this happens. From a buyer's point of view, it's quite an alluring idea that, if the requirement can be expressed as a simple list of components, it will be easy to manage the buying process as a list of items that can be decided simply on price. But things are rarely that simple. Where we are talking about real solutions and co-created value a deal must be based on complete knowledge of a particular situation, and will involve aspects of partnering that can only be revealed through dialog. That's why we use our Collaborative Business Experience. It shifts requests from a transactional to a consultative basis, to determine best value.

'The Collaborative Business Experience help clients, and us, better identify the actual needs, the opportunities accessible to the client, and the value that Capgemini is able uniquely to deliver. It's all about asking questions and discussing requirements – probing, nudging, debating, one-to-one with relevant client personnel and in workshops. Time spent at this stage is never wasted because, if the solution is not achievable to the benefit of both parties, it's not really going to work for anybody. So, not least, this is a great way to qualify sales leads, clarifying situations where Capgemini should withdraw from an opportunity because there is no viable value proposition for us.

'So you can see, clarity around your value proposition at the sales opportunity level is absolutely priceless. Getting it right can save you a lot of blood, sweat, tears and downright loss.'

Strategic value pathway: customer intimacy. Sales mode: consultative

Although the details that follow about creating value propositions can be applied equally to other strategic value pathways, and to transactional sales scenarios, the full power of our argument comes into play in the customer intimacy plus consultative scenario. Here, there is the opportunity to achieve real value leadership.

To do so, you must truly walk in your customers' shoes, understand their businesses, live and breathe their processes, so that you can clearly understand and articulate where you can, and want to, add value in their business.

Leadership and focus are about choosing and adopting a position even if, sometimes, the choice is wrong.

This determines the winners from the losers. If you don't decide and operationalize that decision, you will always be mediocre and end up in no-man's land.

The opposite end of the spectrum from the leadership model is the 'garbage can' model of organizational choice.[6] This views an organization as a garbage can into which various kinds of problems and solutions are dumped by participants as they are generated. The upshot includes the following kinds of outcomes:

- Choices looking for problems.
- Issues looking for decisions.
- Solutions looking for issues to which they might be the answer.
- Decision makers looking for work.

These are scenarios that can certainly allow issues to be aired and in which creativity can flourish, but, because everything remains commercially unfocused, challenges remain unresolved and nothing gets progressed.

A remarkable example of this kind of situation was Xerox PARC (Palo Alto Research Center) in Palo Alto, California, in the early 1970s. It was an amazing place: a hothouse of invention that attracted a galaxy of talent. From it emerged the first personal computer, the graphical user interface (GUI), the idea of distributed computing, the mouse, the idea of a computer screen as a desktop, the application of 'what you see is what you get' screen-to-print output, the concept of object orientation for programming, and more.

How many of these brilliant inventions did Xerox manage to commercialize? None. Zero. Zip. Subsequently, Bill Gates, Steve Jobs and others benefitted hugely from the Xerox PARC endeavours, but the originators themselves, although they may have achieved astonishing levels of intellectual value, achieved hardly any commercial value.

The problem seems to have been a complete disconnect between the perceived sources of value of Xerox as an established copier company, and Xerox as a feisty innovator of what the 1970 CEO, Peter McColough, called the 'architecture of information'.

The Xerox PARC example is extreme because none of the great innovations were commercialized by Xerox. More typically, where a service or solutions company is at least trading, the outcomes of failures of value focus and value leadership of this kind are all too inevitable: growth stalls, margins shrink, and staff and customers go elsewhere.

In these circumstances, as profits slide, management scrambles to introduce temporary quick fixes, to address immediate problems to shore up near-term performance. Companies tweak product and service features to try to make things look fresh, without really doing anything worthwhile. They often increase the levels of customer service staff. And they almost always introduce new marketing promotions and discounting.

But nothing happens, except that the slide continues. Fiddling while Rome burns just makes the situation worse over time and adds complexity. What's needed is an overhaul of the way value is delivered – from strategic intent, via a value proposition-based business model, through a value-focused operating model, and out into value-creation based management and execution.

Notes

1. Here, the value-focused enterprise is introduced. A fuller explanation is given in Chapter 15.
2. http://www.amazonstrategies.com/amazon-101/the-amazon-flywheel-channeladvisor-catalyst-part-iii/.
3. *The Disciplines of Market Leaders*, Michael Treacy and Fred Wiersema, Perseus Publishing, 1995.
4. *The New Solution Selling*, Keith M. Eades, McGraw-Hill, 2004.
5. *Rethinking the Sales Force: Redefining selling to create and capture customer value*, Neil Rackham and John De Vincentis, McGraw-Hill, 1999.
6. *Garbage Can Model of Organizational Choice*, Cohen, March & Olsen, 1972.

4 Creating your value proposition

Marketing is not the art of finding clever ways to dispose of what you make. Marketing is the art of creating genuine customer value. It is the art of helping your customers become better off.

(Philip Kotler, S.C. Johnson & Son Distinguished Professor of International Marketing, Kellogg Graduate School of Management at Northwestern University)

By now, you will have realized that the value proposition concept defines and profoundly influences every part of an enterprise's being and operation. It is at the heart of both strategy and tactics.

The fact is, of course, that every enterprise has a value proposition (that is, customers choose a business because the 'Value = Benefits minus Cost' equation stacks up in some way), otherwise it would not still be in business. The problem is, the value propositions are mostly assumed and implicit rather than thought about and explicit. This is no longer good enough and will not ensure what gets called, these days, high performance.

So, the next part of this book is devoted to helping you create value propositions, taking you in detail through each step of the model that we introduced earlier (see Figure 4.1).

The Value Proposition Builder™ model, as you can see from Figure 4.1, has six elements that lead to the creation of the value proposition you are working on – whether that is at the corporate level or at the customer interface level:

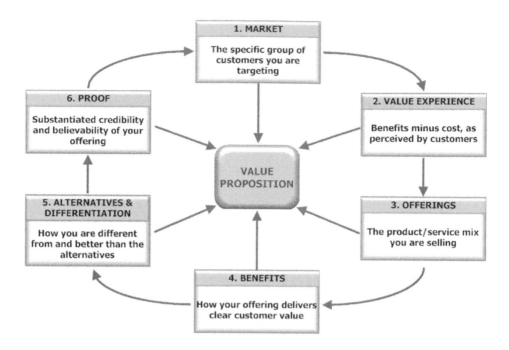

Figure 4.1 The Value Proposition Builder™

- Market: understanding the specific group of customers you want to target.
- Value experience: defining and understanding precisely what it is that your customers value.
- Offerings: mapping, defining, categorizing and managing the life-cycle of your offerings around value.
- Benefits: taking the external and internal views of your value experience and prioritizing them including the cost component (price and customer risk).
- Alternatives and differentiation: what the alternative are to using your organization and how and why you are different (and better) than those alternatives.
- Proof: benefits realization techniques, evidence of your ability to deliver the customers' desired value experience.

Each chapter delves into the inputs – what should be happening at that particular stage of the value proposition building process. In Chapter 11 we will bring it all together into a value proposition template, with timelines and a value proposition statement.

5 Value Proposition Builder: Market

Analysing your market

Pursuing consultative sales is expensive, in terms of time and resources. In 2007, a senior EDS executive calculated that the average cost of pursuing a sales opportunity was $480,000. Win or lose! A top management-level executive in a leading outsourcing provider has said that pursuing an opportunity can cost as much as $5 million. Again, win or lose! Big numbers. Scary numbers. Even where smaller numbers are involved, it is generally true that the cost of pursuing sales opportunities is at an all-time high as measured as a percentage of potential sales revenue, and still rising.

The obvious lesson to take away from this situation is... whatever time you spend on pursuing sales leads and opportunities, plan and allocate it wisely. That means thinking in terms of the quality of the opportunities rather than the quantity. In a contest for a piece of business, winner takes all. There are no prizes for coming second.

However, identifying your best sources of business should be drawn from where you generate most value for customers. We start the value proposition building process by determining the target customer(s). Before you can go anywhere, you need to have a good understanding of who is going to buy your product or service.

Those trained according to the rules of 20th-century marketing will recognize that this is a different start point from the traditional approach. The old model led with 'product' (or 'offer') as the main factor that would determine positioning. People can get very emotional at this stage because a lot of sacred cows are happily grazing in that particular field, and it may have been true a few years ago, but the world and your business and your people have changed, and everything has moved on, so we do have to shoot a few sacred cows every now and again.

We strongly believe in focus. A lot of organizations don't actually like focus when it comes to the market. They have a visceral belief that focus equates to cutting out half of your potential market. They think that focusing down means you are throwing away opportunities rather than increasing your likelihood of winning.

We had exactly this scenario recently. A professional services client was operating across ten market sectors but had agreed that they provided notable value experiences within only four of those sectors. However, the management flatly refused to stop marketing in the remaining six sectors, despite the fact that their value in those sectors was suboptimal, because they firmly believed that 'focus means that you die, because then you'll say no to work'. Sad to say, today it is not doing well as a business.

Define the specific group(s) of customers to target

Because a value proposition defines how an offering will benefit a market segment or customer, and at what cost, it is logical to start by defining the market segment or customer types: who are to be the targeted recipients of the benefits in return for their investment in monetary and other terms?

Key questions to ask yourself

- Where does our organization figure in the marketplace? Is it where we want to be? If not, where would we like to be?
- Which markets or customer types offer the best opportunities for profitable growth? Who are the specific groups of customers we are targeting?

- What are the customer needs? What keeps them awake at night? What are their points of pain?
- Are there discrete market segments?
- What risks do the customers perceive when choosing our organization?
- What's going on in our target market segments? What's hot? What's not?

'Narrow and deep' beats 'broad and shallow'

It is a common misconception that marketing to a wider target market will generate more business. It may work for companies marketing simple, low-cost products that translate well across industries, but when marketing a high-value mix of products, services and solutions, it is critical to focus. Go narrow and deep. By so doing, you will not miss opportunities. Rather, you will be able to make your own opportunities in your chosen markets.

The more focused an approach, the more successful it can be. Focus allows an enterprise to identify the difference between opportunities that meet overall strategic objectives and those that would merely operate tactically in their use of resources or generation of cash flow. Sharp focus enables solutions providers to get clarity around the target markets' 'hot buttons'. You need to:

- Define your markets.
- Map your markets.[1]
- Understand who the decision makers in your markets are and what they purchase.
- Understand why decision makers purchase (and how to meet their needs).
- Form market segments that work for you by combining like-minded decision makers.[2]

Understand how to enter those markets

Any single channel to market is an expensive approach and limits your sales growth capability. Many companies are dependent for sales on a handful of rainmakers. These people rely on their own personal contacts and networks for their sales leads. That means that the company becomes reliant on them. When a rainmaker leaves, all of their expertise goes with them. Rainmakers should only bring in up to a maximum of 20 per cent of your new business revenue. If they bring in more than that, your sales engine is in the hands of too few people. You need knowledge and expertise disseminated throughout your business development community. However, you need to be very clear about how you are providing value to your end customers, which is what the following chapters will help you to uncover.

We were told that the network economy would eliminate intermediaries—disintermediation, ecosystems, partners, alliances—enabling a direct path from producer to customer. This was a misjudgement of the nature of intermediaries and networks. Intermediaries survive by adding value. Identify those partners who can add the most value to the delivery of your sales and marketing objectives. Actively manage your partners with agreed objectives, terms of reference including roles and responsibilities, measurement, and regular, frequent review and planning meetings.

More reasons to be market-focused

In addition to the general reasons for market and segment focus, there are specific factors related to the cost of pursuing opportunities (an opportunity is a qualified sales lead).

Research shows that the cost of pursuing sales is now at an all-time high and still rising. In order to maximize return on investment (ROI), it therefore makes obvious sense to make highly informed, excellent choices about which opportunities to pursue. Rifle shot is better than scattergun. But be aware of a couple of classic traps:

- Generally, the more opportunities salespeople have, the safer they feel.
- Many sales people look for opportunities based on ease, not strategic value.

So, watch out for these pitfalls, be ruthless in your selection of sales opportunities, and go narrow and deep.

Critical thinking

All too often we see that once the segmentation exercise starts, paralysis by analysis creeps in, with those responsible for market segmentation spending much of their time researching, studying and dissecting the target markets for which they are responsible. Thus we see the most beautiful and detailed pieces of market analysis created without any grasp of what is actually happening 'out there' with your actual customers. In other words, this extensive analysis starts to cut off the business from its customers – a crucial mistake when focusing on delivering value. Customers need to be at the heart of your organization.

Once you have identified those areas of the market where you create value for your customers, you then need to spend time with a range of 'typical' current customers who are able to articulate what that value is, in detail. In the next chapter, we'll examine precisely that step in the process.

Notes

1. A full and excellent explanation of market mapping, and the segmentation process, is given in *Market Segmentation: How to do it, how to profit from it*, Malcolm McDonald and Ian Dunbar, Elsevier Butterworth-Heinemann, 2004 and reprints.
2. A market segment is defined by McDonald and Dunbar as: 'a group of customers within a market who share a similar level of interest in the same, or comparable, set of needs'. The first component of a market segment is, therefore, the list of needs that the individuals in that segment regard as important to them when selecting which competing offer to buy.

6 Value Proposition Builder: The value experience

As we've already said, value, like beauty, is in the eye of the beholder. In other words, you can aim to deliver what you perceive and believe to be value. What is actually valuable is what your customers say they value.

Focus on customer experience delivers profit

The basic concept of customer experience is generally understood – that price and functionality are no longer enough (if they ever were!). Organizations around the world are starting to focus on how customers experience the interactions with them, not least of which is a strong correlation between customer experience and customer loyalty.

Companies that have a definition for customer experience and use this definition in everyday decision making are more likely to exceed profit and revenue goals than those that don't, according to a study.

'Finding the Performance Pay-off in Customer Experience' in 2008 surveyed 644 business leaders at all levels of leadership, organizational areas and across industries, from health care to manufacturing. The research was designed and conducted by Aveus, a US-based strategy consultancy.

Definitions of customer experience vary widely. The study breaks new ground by surveying business leaders about how their organizations define customer experience and which definitions yield the biggest performance pay-off. The survey showed that 26 per cent of companies with a definition of customer experience reported exceeding profit targets, while only 14 per cent of those without a definition could report the same.

Furthermore, the survey showed that organizations with the strongest use of customer experience in daily decision making report the strongest operating results, with 67 per cent reporting meeting or exceeding revenue targets; 65 per cent met or exceeded profit targets. These organizations use customer experience as a planned strategy for achieving performance.

Peer Insight reported a three-year study (2004–07) of 40 Fortune 500 companies – 'Blueprint: The Discipline of Service Innovation'. The results show that companies that focused upon customer experience design outperformed the S&P 500 by a 10:1 margin.

Through the use of customer experience, and using it in a structured value proposition building model, then linking to financial and customer performance, business leaders will be able to make the operating decisions that hold the strongest potential for performance and profit pay-off in their organization.

The value of research

Many organizations believe that finding out what a customer really values is a daunting task. However, if you put yourself in the customer's shoes and think what you would look for, it's a good starting point. Think about product or service needs, of course, but also think about support, service quality, relationships, knowledge, skills required to deliver, how easy (or not) it is to buy from you, and so on. Those organizations that start the process find that the more interviews, assessments and research they do on value, the easier and more valuable they become.

The 'no research' option

Almost unbelievably, there are many organizations out there that have never researched their customers' needs, wants, desires and expectations of value. These organizations go to market and deliver services and products based almost entirely on strong beliefs about the value and attractiveness of what they do. Oh, there may be some lip service paid to research via the purchase of some secondary third-party reports, but they don't talk or listen to what is truly valued by their customers... often until it's too late.

Worthless research

Frequently, the more common issue with research is that organizations seem to commission lots of research, but still have no idea about what their customers want. The key question to ask in this instance is: 'Is this research actually telling me what I need to know?' Customer satisfaction surveys can be the main culprit here. Your customers may well answer what you ask them on a scale of 1–5, but are you finding out what they *really* value? Truly?

Types of research

There are a number of ways you can undertake research with your customers. There isn't a magic bullet here. You need to understand what you're trying to find out, how big a sample of your customers you want to take, what your budget is and what your timescale is.

Here are a few research techniques for you to think about:

- face-to-face interviews;
- telephone interviews;
- focus groups;
- online surveys;
- written surveys.

Become the customer

Few organizations truly understand their customers' experiences well enough. Managers must learn what their customers really want by 'becoming the customer'. Try to identify with your customers – learn their goals, needs, desires, wants and problems in a way that you firmly and emotionally believe in. The key is not to imagine what you would want if you were in the customer's situation but rather to imagine you actually are the customer.

Spend time with your customer

For example, try to explore how your customers behave – especially if they are significantly different from you. If your customer is, for example, a plastics manufacturer, you need to spend time on the factory floor and experiencing the challenges of the people in that factory. Especially if you don't really want to.

Experience not buying process

You should also spend time understanding the relevant experiences your customers value. Rather than focusing on what buyers and influencers are looking for, try to understand what experiences the customer organization will derive.

Avoid intermediaries

Don't try to avoid becoming the customer, by employing such techniques as user groups, focus groups, industry gurus, futurologists, etc, all of which may well not be ahead of the market but rather off the pace. To manage an organization that bases itself on understanding what customers really want, then, you need to relinquish these intermediaries.

Be in your customer's business

Don't let your business define what you do. You need to define how your service or product is utilized and then focus on delivering that experience.

Observation

If possible, observe how your customers use your products or services. If not, then ask your customers to shut their eyes and describe how they use your products or services from memory – it's the next best thing to actually being there.

Understanding versus listening

Customers don't always know what experiences they would value, even if you ask them. Customers don't spend their time imagining what product or service, along with its value to them, is going to be desired. This is why customer listening programmes should not be used to define value experiences, product/service development or, indeed, any major strategic move. This advice absolutely does not intend to be disrespectful to customers. You should talk and listen to them. However, becoming the customer is about uncovering what would be most valuable to customers and that your organization can deliver profitably.

Understand competing alternatives

By becoming your customer, you can explore what alternatives are available to your customers and thus understand your competitive landscape more fully.

One of our clients was an automotive component manufacturing plant in the United Kingdom. In the 1990s, one of their directors would take the entire shop floor and office workforce to visit a key customer's assembly plant as part of a total quality management (TQM) program. The people would spend all day with the customer's assembly line staff, talking to them, understanding what their jobs entailed and every aspect of how their product was used. Not only were the staff members encouraged to build relationships at all levels with the customer's staff, but they were also encouraged to care enough about their job to ask questions, be inquisitive and problem-solve. The director would ask each person to hold in their minds the question: 'How can we make the customer's experience of using our product even better?' This question applied to every single person in the manufacturing organization.

   As a result, the timing and frequency of deliveries improved, size and shape of packaging, the commercial model and sometimes the actual product design was altered. All of the changes were determined through working as a team and with the customer. None of the work pandered to unreasonable customer demand – only aspects of the whole product were changed, when it was profitable to do so – a subject we explore in the next chapter. All of this was achieved in a heavily unionized factory, so just think what could be achieved in a professional services organization, for example!

Ascertaining what the customer values

Value challenge

Customers sometimes do not have an accurate understanding of what it is they value. They probably haven't thought about it in such terms, and customer satisfaction surveys won't find this out for you. What will find this out is having a conversation or, if you prefer, skilled qualitative research questioning.

We recommend using a third party to hold a series of face-to-face business conversations with your most valued customers. These must be conducted by good, qualitative business research professionals. Some organizations are hesitant about using third parties, thinking they'll be able to send in their own people to ask questions, but to get both total honesty from your customers and an impartial and unbiased view of the value experience, it is imperative that no one from your own organization is involved in the one-to-one interviews. It is also important not to use a set questionnaire. What's needed is a flexible framework that experienced, highly business-aware interviewers can use appropriately to draw out relevant information. That's why it is important that those doing the interviewing are top-notch, senior business professionals.

These people will know how to ask the right questions in the right way and to follow and interrogate conversational leads from your customers. Good interviewers know when to listen and when to ask further questions. They get more, much more, out of your customers that way.

It is also important to interview members of staff to get the internal perspective on how staff members believe they deliver value to your customers. This allows you to find any gaps between the perception and the reality of customer experience.

Value is experienced both qualitatively and quantitatively. We suggest using topic guides to structure the discussions so as to extract information around: perceived value to the individual and their organization; market issues; competitors; offers; areas of strength; and any constructive feedback the interviewee wishes to give. The questions themselves are valid whether they are asked of a customer or a member of staff. The correlation of responses provides fascinating insight into your organization's value.

You need to ascertain needs:

- What precisely are your customers' needs?
- What do your customers value?
- Of these, which areas have priority over others, and why?
- Which competitors or alternatives measure up to these areas of value?
- How does your organization stack up?
- What are the benefits and costs experienced by your customers in the process?

You also need to ascertain what experience they wanted and have experienced. Were they looking for a more transactional experience? (That is, cheap, quick, low-touch, no relationship.) Or were they looking for a consultative experience? (That is, high interaction, strong relationships, advice, commensurate value-pricing.) Were they looking for a variety of ways of working with your organization?

You should ask:

- What are the most important factors when your customers are looking to purchase [product/service]?
- Who is the best supplier of this experience? What do you specifically like about this supplier?
- Do you always like to have a relationship with your supplier?
- What do you value beyond price/cost?
- What could we do to improve your experience of working with us?

The value interview

As stated earlier, our preferred technique is the face-to-face interview. As a mechanism for understanding value, it's hard to beat. In order to elicit the information you need to understand your customers' experience of your value, we suggest the following topic areas of questioning by your third-party questioners. The interviews should last no more than 30 minutes to avoid 'burning' relationships:

1. Background to relationship.
2. Value.

3. Cost (including price and risk).
4. Offerings.
5. Marketplace.
6. Competitors and alternatives.
7. Recommendations and suggestions.

Background to relationship

This is to set up the context for the interview: to set the ground rules and to get the relationship between interviewer and interviewee started. By enquiring about the background to the relationship between the supplier and the customer the selection process can be discovered – for example, was the choice to use the supplier an active one, or was the relationship inherited?

Value

In this area of questioning, it is vital that the interviewer probes and tests the responses without leading the interviewee. It is here that both qualitative and quantitative questions and responses can be extracted. Very often an interviewee will respond either solely qualitatively or solely quantitatively. But in a business-to-business (B2B) environment it is vital to understand both types of information and to understand the relative importance of each; so the interviewer must be briefed carefully and probe to elicit both types of value experience.

Cost (including price and risk)

Value is often perceived against purchase price, so understanding a customer's general attitude to price and pricing is critical. It's also usually weighed up against the risk factors involved. Here are some example questions.:

General

- How would you describe the value that [supplier] has brought to a) your business and b) you, personally?
- Any particular areas they need to work on? Key weaknesses?
- Any particular areas they need to promote? Key strengths?

Price

- How big a factor is price in your decision-making process?
- How does [supplier] rate in terms of price?
- If you had a choice between cost/price versus value-add, which way would you go? Why?

Risk

- Did you perceive any risks when you chose this supplier?
- If so, what were they?

And back to the general...

- How could [supplier] position itself going forward?

What do we mean by risk?

Risks come in all sorts of shapes and sizes but they can be classified under three main headings: rational, political and emotional. you'll find more about this in Chapter 12, 'Message development' (because, obviously, your messages need, among other things, to counter risks), but, for now, here are some initial thoughts.

Rational (logic/detail/content)

Rational risks are fairly straightforward and must be measured. For example, 'Is this quoted delivery date reliable?' Or, 'Introducing this new offer/product/service carries risk. What can I do to mitigate it?'

Political (organizational)

Organizations can be tricky beasts and sometimes people find it necessary to watch their backs. It's the kind of situation that gives rise to the, 'Nobody ever got fired for hiring IBM/Microsoft/ Accenture...' sort of thing.

Emotional (personal)

These are factors that touch a buyer personally: for example, 'I've never used this supplier before. Am I making the best decision?'

Offerings

The next chapter deals with your offerings in detail. To understand the value of your offerings, questions in this area must probe what it was your customers thought they were buying, and whether this is what they actually received. It's a great opportunity to understand which of your offerings are fresh and to the point, and which are tired and should be put out to pasture. Here are some example questions:

- What was it about the supplier's offering(s) that you found most valuable?
- How have you reacted to the supplier's newest offering? Does it stack up favourably against their old one(s)?

Marketplace

As we examined in the previous chapter, it is important to understand where your business is going to come from and what the key issues are for that particular sector of the market. Here's the opportunity to test and validate your earlier analysis. Example questions:

- What are your core business goals?
- Are you achieving them?
- What keeps you awake at night?
- What do you regard as the current priority issues for your business /your sector?
- What trends do you see coming in this sector?
- Looking forward, do you see any changes to these – what do you believe will become critical over the next three years?
- Knowing [supplier] as you do, do you believe it can provide services to meet these needs?
- What do they need to do to achieve that?

Competitors and alternatives

It's tough out there and only the most naive of us would imagine that we're the only game in town. Your customers very often will choose an in-house alternative or, that biggest competitor of them all, the 'do-nothing' option.

When examining competition, it's always good to find points of differentiation (to make your organization special and significant) but also to find points of parity (to ensure you're not on your own in left-field). Here are some example questions:

- Did you think about doing this work in-house?
- Did you think about not doing this work at all?
- From your perspective, who are the top three companies? Why do you say that?
- How is [supplier] different from these other organizations?
- How does their pricing compare with [supplier]?
- In your experience, working with other businesses in this area, which do you really enjoy working with and why? Is there anything [supplier] can learn from them?

Recommendations and suggestions

It's always wise to give interviewees an opportunity to express themselves freely. They may have something they are burning to say that hasn't been picked up in earlier questioning. It may be a specific plaudit or it may be a brickbat.

On one occasion, we were interviewing the head of a major corporation over a significant piece of management consulting work. During the bulk of the interview he gave thoughtful, considered responses and articulated the value of the piece of consulting work very clearly. However, at the end of the interview, he had a short and pithy outburst about the consulting firm's e-mail footers. They had laid out all their awards and credentials at the bottom of every e-mail. This had irritated the CEO so much that he simply had to vent his irritation over the excess paper generated when an e-mail trail was printed out and the perceived arrogance of the consulting firm 'showing off'. He'd mentioned it at the time to his programme manager but this had clearly been treated as inconsequential. The result? He took his business elsewhere. Over an e-mail footer. Actually, it was about being ignored – he felt that his requests should be listened to and to him this demonstrated a lack of listening and a lack of customer care.

Here are some example questions:

- What three things do you believe [supplier] should do going forward?
- Is there anything you would like to add about this company's value to you?

Output

At the end of the third-party interviews, it is important that there is a clear, consolidated report that gives both a concise executive summary of the findings from the customer interviews, plus recommendations, as well as detailed customer feedback notes.

Summary

The research you have now undertaken about customer needs and experiences of value will provide significant input into the development of your value proposition. Having completed the value proposition development process thus far you will now have an understanding of your target market, and the value experience that you are able to deploy.

The next phase is to understand, define and refine your offerings.

7 Value Proposition Builder: Offerings

With your market choices made, and value experience identified, you are in a position to work on your offerings. This is an important and substantial task in itself.

To start the process, the most important thing to keep in mind is that unless you are a new start-up you already have offerings. It is so easy to get caught up in the excitement of thinking about new offerings, and developing the process to bring them about, that offerings that already exist can get sidelined. It's just that they may not be identified and understood. So, your start point should be the identification and categorization of your existing offerings.

In fact, the order of your focus needs to be:

Step 1. Understand and categorize the offerings that you currently have.
Step 2. Put in place an offering management process (OMP), including the people to manage it. This should include an innovation and new offering development process.
Step 3. Using your OMP, identify where your offerings are in the offering life cycle (see Figure 13.6), including those that should be retired.
Step 4. Develop new offerings.

Bear in mind that you may only need to complete Step 1 above. You may not need to go through Steps 2, 3 or 4. Therefore, we have focused this chapter on Step 1, because this is done during the value proposition building stage. Step 2 is highlighted in Chapter 13 on implementation, as are Steps 3 and 4. These last two steps are also covered and written about extensively in other excellent books and articles.

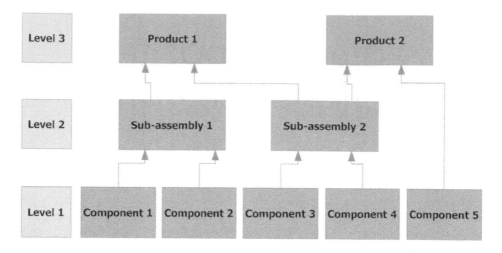

Figure 7.1   Bill of materials

When you have categorized and labelled your existing offering portfolio, you are able to see where each offering sits in the lifecycle. Not least, this will indicate which offerings are reaching the end of their useful life and need to be retired or be extended in some way. This will also suggest how exposed you may be to threats, and indicate requirements for new offering development.

Let's consider these points step by step.

Step 1. Categorize your current portfolio

We tend to think that it is easy for manufacturing and product companies to categorize their products, but more difficult for service companies to do so. There is a tendency for those of us in the services sector – particularly in consulting – to think that, because our offerings are less tangible, they are more complicated and somehow superior to the manufacturing and product equivalents. There's a certain intellectual snobbery about it. But it's nonsense.

If you are a service provider, or provide a product-service amalgam, think of your offerings as products (for a short while, at least). That way, you'll likely find it a lot easier to define the components – the bill of materials, so to speak – that go to make up the whole. So think of building offerings like building products. Level 1 is the bottom-level

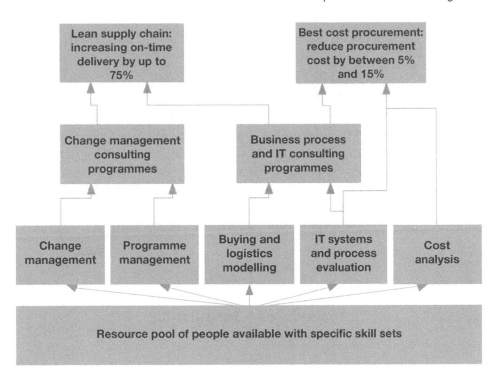

Figure 7.2 Example bill of materials for a supply chain consultancy (services organization)

component level. Level 2 could be offering A to market segment Z and Level 3 could be offering B to market segment W.

The kind of structure is shown in Figure 7.1. You are more likely to sell higher volume but less value at Level 1 and lower volume but higher value at Level 3. To make it more tangible, Figure 7.2 shows an example as it might apply in a supply chain consulting organization.

Only when this mapping has been completed – and it may be quite a lengthy exercise – will you be able to position your components, offers, solutions, and co-created value onto the Value Pyramid™, as explained next.

It is our experience that the whole of this exercise is best carried out using workshops: create hypotheses and workshop through with your offering managers or solutions leads.

The whole product or whole service

Although we have asked you to think of your services as products, we mean you to think of the whole product (Figure 7.3). The 'whole product' concept was first written about by Theodore Levitt[1] and also used in the seminal *Crossing the Chasm.*[2] The idea is that there is a gap between the marketing promise made to the customer and the ability of the delivered product or service to fulfil that promise. For that gap to be overcome, the product must be augmented by a variety of services and ancillary products to become 'the whole product'. We have modified this idea and used it in our benefits map in Chapter 8.

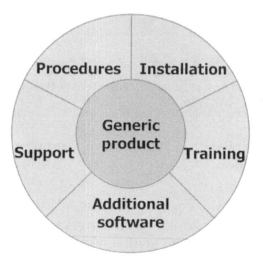

Figure 7.3 A whole product map for a technology product

Source: modified from *Crossing the Chasm,* Geoffrey Moore, HarperCollins, 1991

The notion of the whole product is very important in both product and services organizations. Geoffrey Moore's assertion in *Crossing the Chasm* is that you need to convince the early majority to purchase (the folks after the early adopters in the 'diffusion of innovation' curve[3]). To do this you need to build the whole product – a complete solution to a real-life problem, with all the necessary pieces in place to deliver all the value of the solution. And for technology companies, this is not about delivering the technology but rather about delivering the whole value experience.

Moore's book has just as much value today as it did in 1991. The entire thesis was to identify the marketing problems that keep a lot of technology companies from becoming business successes. Most of these challenges still exist today because of a focus on the technology rather than a full understanding, building and articulation of the value proposition.

Map to the Value Pyramid™

Having identified your offering portfolio, map the offerings to the Value Pyramid™ that we introduced earlier. You may recall that the basic components are component, offer, solution and co-created value, and that the nature of the sales processes around each of these categories changes profoundly, as indicated in Figures 7.4 and 7.5.

Figure 7.6 shows an example offering portfolio map for a market intelligence consultancy: we have envisaged a company that offers a range of research and analysis services to its clients.

Once this mapping is complete, it is far easier to see the way forward because you are able to identify:

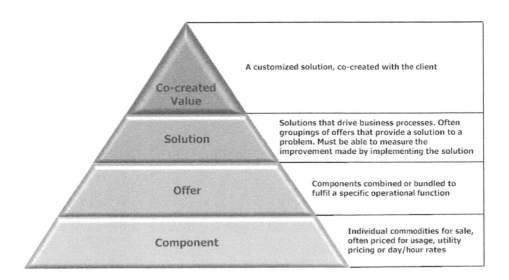

Figure 7.4 The Value Pyramid™: showing units of sale

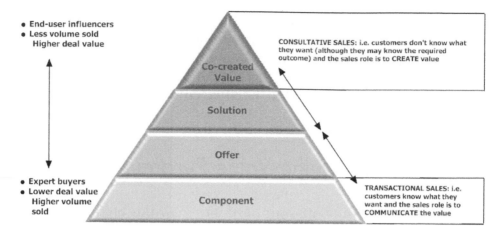

Figure 7.5 The Value Pyramid™: showing the transactional versus consultative sales axis

Figure 7.6 The Value Pyramid™: mapped with offerings – market intelligence consultancy

- what offers can be grouped together to form new solutions or higher-value offerings;
- what offerings in one part of the business can be combined with other offerings from other areas (sectors or technical lines) to create new offerings;

- what pricing needs to be used with which offerings and what level of profitability is required;
- how each type or group of offerings should be sold, ie which lend themselves to low cost of sale, automated or transactional selling, and which to high-touch, problem solving, high value-added consultative selling;
- to whom should each offering be sold – offerings suited to transactional selling will be targeted to expert buyers (eg procurement experts); whereas solutions and high-value offerings will normally involve consultative selling with more senior management (eg chief executive officer and other senior executives), who, although they may know generally what they want to achieve, will need value-creation support to help them shape the solution;
- how long it will take to sell the respective offerings – offerings lower down the value pyramid generally have a shorter sales cycle than those nearer the top.

Profitability

We also recommend a radical review of the profitability of your products and services. Key metrics are the sales volumes that each product or service generates, your stock requirements, the gross profit of each unit of sale or service, and the commercial terms with both your suppliers and customers. You should use this information to rank your products and services in order of their ability to generate profit and positive cash flow. Having identified your best products, you should then examine whether your sales and marketing approach needs to be refined.

During the 2008/09 recession, a travel industry client reduced its offering down to a narrow niche of cruises and then focused its marketing effort and management time on ensuring these were profitable and generated cash quickly. Although there was a temporary fall in sales, the company returned to positive cash flow and profit within a matter of weeks.

Notes

1. *The Marketing Imagination*, Theodore Levitt, Simon & Schuster, 1986.
2. *Crossing The Chasm*, Geoffrey A. Moore, HarperCollins, 1991.
3. *Diffusion of Innovations*, Everett Rogers, Simon & Schuster International, 5th Revised edition 2003.

8 Value Proposition Builder: Benefits

By the time you reach this stage, benefits analysis, you will have reached an understanding of your market, examined the value experienced by existing customers, and looked at the offer in considerable detail. A key advantage of this work is getting rid of myths that may have built up within the organization over time. Value cannot be based on delusions. It is essential to understand the reality.

Benefits should be based tightly upon experiences of value by customers and staff. Benefits statements must not be platitudes or bland statements of how you deliver your product or service. Nor must they drift into characteristics of your brand or how you run your business. Phrases such as 'We're here for the long haul' or 'We're responsive and flexible' are undifferentiated and, frankly, meaningless to most of your intended audiences. Keep your benefits aligned to experiences of value.

To extract these benefits, you need to take the value statements given by the customers interviewed to ascertain the experience of working with your organization. Staff interviews also provide significant insight into how your people perceive the value of their work – and also highlight whether you have gaps between your organization and your customers when it comes to value experiences. But how do you make them practically helpful, functional and real? Key phrases that are found from both within and outside the organization – ie where both customers and staff agree on areas of significant value – are going to be critical and will be at the heart of your value proposition. So the next step is to create a benefits map (Figure 8.1) to enable you to split out the core service purchased from the benefits that customers expect to receive, and the benefits that are additional to expectation

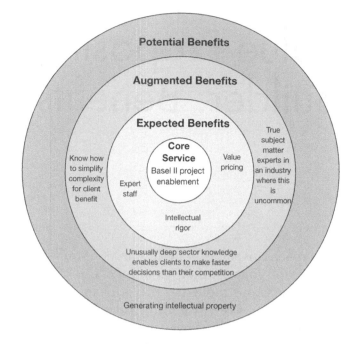

Figure 8.1 The benefits map

Source: modified from 'The Whole Product Model' in *The Marketing Imagination*, Theodore Levitt, Simon & Schuster, 1986.

(augmented), and finally those where potential benefits could be realized (potential).

Expected benefits

Items in the 'expected benefits' circle are usually, frankly, hygiene factors: customers generally expect to experience such things as high-quality people, reliability, timeliness, good pricing, responsiveness to client demands, and so on. It's a fact, however, that far too many organizations cite such things as timeliness, good pricing and responsiveness as if they were significant differentiators. They may have been differentiating once upon a time but it is difficult to imagine any sector where, for example, 'high quality' is now seen as anything other than a given. It's the minimum value experience.

Augmented or additional benefits

Once you have separated out the expected benefits, you will find yourself working with additional, or 'augmented', benefits. These are areas where clients were pleasantly surprised, even delighted, to receive value and benefits that they hadn't expected. These are the benefits that will be the most useful to you when understanding why you are providing different and significant value to your customers. In other words, it's the maximum value experience.

Potential benefits

In the outermost ring of the benefits map, you occasionally find potential benefits. This is where customers proffer suggestions of benefits that may be coming from the relationship with your organization. Occasionally, these may include the creation of intellectual property (IP). In other words – room for growth.

Translating benefits into messages

The key deliverable from this stage of the process is the creation of messages for use by the whole organization. This is dealt with in more detail in Chapter 12, but we'll take a quick walk past this area now.

Messages based on benefits drawn from customer experience are based on truth and reality, and not on assumptions or ideas generated by marketing or sales people. The latter are rarely bought into by an organization or its customers. Customers have no vested interest in saying anything but the truth of their experience, hence your messaging will be based on truth and will be valid internally and externally and will be applicable to market, sales and operations. Where customers and staff have independently agreed on areas of value found in the augmented/additional circle, they will be your most important value credentials.

To generate messages from the Value Proposition Builder™ process, the key is to extract the qualitative and quantitative benefits from the augmented and potential rings, and map them on to a two by two matrix for further refinement. The *x*-axis is 'value to customer'. The *y*-axis is 'differentiation from competition'. Messages ending up in the top right-hand quadrant (high value to customer and high differentiation from competition) are, by default, your most impactful messages (as shown in Figure 12.1 in Chapter 12).

Value experience is critical

At the risk of labouring the point here, the benefits statements that you place on to your benefits map really must be based on customer experiences of value. Too often we find descriptions of services, brand characteristics or vague statements that sound OK on first reading but, in reality, are meaningless to customers. Particular favourites in this platitudes category often come from the important but ill-defined areas of quality, service and customer satisfaction. Everyone knows these are important and so they tend to throw these and related phrases into benefits statements without defining precisely what they mean to the customer.

The worst thing, though, is when benefits statements are reduced to such platitudes that no one can actually argue with them. They're just bland and offend no one. This often stems from an organization where no one can agree what the real value of the business is and the hapless and despairing marketing department takes the path of least resistance to 'getting something out there'. The only way to cut through the blandness is to ensure that customer value experience is the basis for your benefits statements.

The 'So what?' challenge

Apply the 'So what?' challenge to every statement. For example, 'Our people are highly qualified' just doesn't stand up to the 'So What?' test. Whereas 'Our highly qualified people ensure you submit your tax return on time, with no errors and in full compliance with Revenue requirements, while ensuring you pay an appropriate and equitable amount of tax' does pass the 'So what?' test.

The value difference

Once you have split out your expected, augmented and potential benefits and are clear about what is most valued by your customers, you will need to ensure that they are compared with what the customers' viable alternatives are. After all, you are unlikely to be the only game in town. And how do you stack up against that killer alternative, the in-house option?

So, it is important to examine all of the alternatives. Ask the question: 'Why should the customer use our offering as opposed to using: a) one of our competitors or b) doing it themselves?' This will force you to compare your value with your competitors' and other alternatives.

You may find that you have several points of difference and a point of parity with your nearest competitor. This is a perfectly valid finding and can legitimize you with your customers if you are operating in a highly competitive market space.

We'll examine more about alternatives and differentiation in the next chapter.

9 Value Proposition Builder: Alternatives and differentiation

By this stage of the process, many things have become clear. The outdated, the irrelevant and accumulated debris have been stripped away and focus has been drawn to your market, the value you bring your customers, how your offering combines to create optimal value for you and your customers, and how to distil the benefits you bring into something useable for you.

The reason we suggest waiting until now to examine your competitors and competitive landscape is that if the question is asked about competitors at the beginning of the process, it is almost impossible to get a realistic and considered answer until the dust of history has been brushed away. Perhaps now your value has been realigned your competitor set may have changed. Sometimes your competitive landscape changes almost without you noticing.

Most importantly, though, the reason you must never start a value process by analysing your competition is because you must examine what your customers really value before doing anything. This is why the traditional SWOT analysis shouldn't be done until this stage of the process. Strengths, Weaknesses, Opportunities and Threats can only be fully identified when you can truly understand what your customers value, how you can deliver this and how you can beat the external and internal competitors and alternatives. The same holds true for benchmarking: without examining the customer value set before doing a competitor benchmarking exercise, you will benchmark in a customer-free vacuum. This can lead you wildly astray.

To maintain your market share, or to gain market share, leadership, customer base or whatever is your driving strategy, you must understand why you are 'special' – which is what the previous chapters have examined. Now that you are clear about your market space and the value you're bringing to your customers, you must ensure you keep your competitors tracked. This tracking does not mean undertaking the usual, fact-driven competitor intelligence-gathering exercise, where reams of data and benchmarking facts are compiled – usually in an impressive binder which sits gathering dust after the first read. Rather, we're talking about understanding how your competitors deliver their value.

It is at this point you need to ask yourself a few more questions:

- Which alternatives can deliver the best value to my customers?
- In what time frame?
- Are my competitors able to deliver this value cheaper, faster and better than my organization?
- What makes my organization different from and better than my competition?
- What does the overall competitive landscape look like?
- How do my offerings give me competitive advantage with my customers? And how can I combine them to best effect to marginalize my competitors?

One way of examining your competitive landscape is to map out what the competing marketplace alternatives are. An example for a business process improvement organization is given in Figure 9.1.

By keeping abreast of what your customers value and what your competitors are offering, you can ensure that your offerings are constantly refreshed to deliver what you can do well, and that it will take time for your competitors to follow. You can either combine your new elements with your old elements to make a bundled offering, or offer these new services separately or as add-on, high-value stand-alone elements to ensure you fully understand where to invest.

Ultimately, though, be aware that you are not competing against your competitors' services or products or offerings. You are competing against their value propositions. You need to understand how your competitors are delivering, or intend to deliver, their value experiences to the customer. To do that, you need to do your best to keep abreast of everything that your customer values and what your competitors are providing. You may be concerned that you are part of a fast-changing

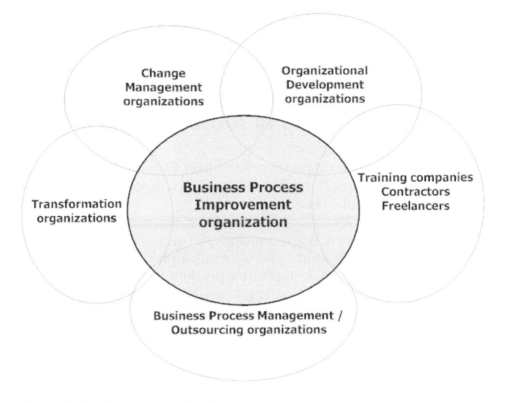

Figure 9.1 Competitor landscape map

market, such as technology, and that there's no way you can keep up with what's happening in your competitors' businesses. Bear in mind, though, that value does not change as fast as technology. Products and services inevitably change faster than the way customers experience value. This is what you're competing against.

However, as often as not, customers perceive the best competing alternative to using an external supplier as being the in-house or 'do-it-yourself' option. As your customers become more expert, it's up to you to keep your offerings fresh and provide a superior experience of the value you bring. One way of doing this is by ensuring that you blend the experience gained across all customers and focus it on each of your customers, as well as hiring fresh new talent into your organization and, ultimately, keeping several steps ahead of both your own customers and your external competition.

The most common alternative, though, is the 'do-nothing' option. It is almost always easy to cite budgetary or other operational constraints as good reasons for doing nothing. You need to be compelling, articulate and, above all, smart about how you convey your value.

Assessing alternatives and differentiation by looking at substitutes

It is important to understand that alternatives may not just be the usual suspects, the obvious candidates. Here are two pieces that illuminate different aspects of the issue.

First, Michael Porter on 'substitutes': Porter, author of 'The five competitive forces that shape strategy'[1], is one of the world's most prolific and respected strategy gurus. A substitute performs the same or a similar function as an industry's product by a different means. Videoconferencing is a substitute for travel. Plastic is a substitute for aluminium. E-mail is a substitute for express mail. Sometimes, the threat of substitution is downstream or indirect, when a substitute replaces a buyer industry's product. For example, lawn care products and services are threatened when multifamily homes in urban areas substitute for single-family homes in the suburbs. Software sold to travel agents is threatened when airline and travel websites substitute for them.

Substitutes are always present, but they are easy to overlook because they may appear to be very different from the industry's product. It is a substitute to do without, to purchase a used product rather than a new one, or to do it yourself (bring the service or product in-house).

When the threat of substitutes is high, industry profitability suffers. Substitute products or services limit an industry's profit potential by placing a ceiling on prices. If an industry does not distance itself from substitutes through product performance, marketing, or other means, it will suffer in terms of profitability – and often growth potential.

Substitutes not only limit profits in normal times, they also reduce the bonanza an industry can reap in good times. In emerging economies, for example, the surge in demand for wired telephone lines has been capped as many consumers opt to make a mobile phone their first and only phone.

The threat of a substitute is high if:

- It offers an attractive price–performance trade-off to the industry's product. The better the relative value of the substitute, the tighter is the lid on an industry's profit potential. For example, conventional providers of long-distance telephone service have suffered from the advent of inexpensive internet-based phone services such as Vonage and Skype. Similarly, video rental outlets are struggling with the emergence of cable and satellite video-on-demand services, online video rental services such as Netflix, and the rise of internet video sites like Google's YouTube.
- The buyer's cost of switching to the substitute is low. Switching from a proprietary, branded drug to a generic drug usually involves minimal costs, for example, which is why the shift to generics (and the fall in prices) is so substantial and rapid.

Strategists should be particularly alert to changes in other industries that may make them attractive substitutes when they were not before. Improvements in composite materials, for example, allowed them to substitute for steel in many car components. In this way, technological changes or competitive discontinuities in seemingly unrelated businesses can have a major impact on industry profitability. Of course the substitution threat can also shift in favor of an industry, which bodes well for its future profitability and growth potential.

Second, we consider the example of Intuit from W. Chan Kim and Renée Mauborgne, perhaps best known for their Blue Ocean Strategy,[2] (the means to create uncontested, 'blue-water' market space away from the 'blood-red', shark-infested waters of densely competing market spaces).

Looking across alternative industries to create new market space: the case of Intuit[3]

Similar to NetJets and Home Depot, Intuit, the company that changed the way individuals and small businesses manage their finances, also got its insight into value innovation by thinking about how customers make trade-offs across substitutes. Its Quicken software allows individuals to organize, understand, and manage their personal finances. Every household goes through the monthly drudgery of paying bills. Hence, in principle, personal financial software should be a big and broad market. Yet before Quicken, few people used software to automate this tedious and repetitive task. At the time of Quicken's release in 1984, the 42 existing software packages for personal finance had yet to crack the market.

Why? As Intuit founder Scott Cook recalls: 'The greatest competitor we saw was not in the industry. It was the pencil. The pencil is a really tough and resilient substitute. Yet the entire industry had overlooked it.'

Asking why buyers trade across substitutes led Intuit to an important insight. The pencil had two decisive advantages over computerized solutions: amazingly low cost and extreme simplicity of use. At prices of around $300, existing software packages were too expensive. They were also hard to use, presenting intimidating interfaces full of accounting terminology.

Intuit focused on bringing out both the decisive advantages that the computer has over the pencil – speed and accuracy – and the decisive advantages that the pencil has over computers – simplicity of use and low price – and eliminated or reduced everything else. With its user-friendly interface that resembles the familiar checkbook, Quicken is far faster and more accurate than the pencil, yet almost as simple to use. Intuit eliminated the accounting jargon and all the sophisticated features that were part of the industry's conventional wisdom about 'how we compete'. It offered instead only the few basic functions that most customers use. Simplifying the software cut costs. Quicken retailed at about $90, a 70 per cent price drop. Neither the pencil nor other software packages could compete with Quicken's divergent value curve. Quicken created breakthrough value and re-created the industry, and has expanded the market some hundredfold.

There is a further lesson to be drawn from the way Intuit thought about and looked across substitutes. In looking for other products or services that could perform the same function as its own, Intuit could have focused on private accounting firms that handle finances for individuals. But when there is more than one substitute, it is smart to explore the ones with the greatest volumes in usage as well as in monetary value. Framed that way, more Americans use pencils than accountants to manage their personal finances.

What's your difference?

When you have done your homework, there is a neat way to assess and summarize your points of difference using a simple matrix. It looks something like Figure 9.2.

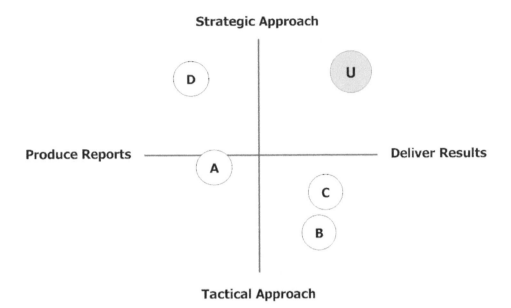

Figure 9.2   Sample points of difference matrix

Note: U = your organization. A, B, C and D are competitor organizations

The matrix enables you to plot your own organization and competitors in terms of their performance against various criteria. This example relates to consultancy of some kind. 'Produce reports' is shorthand for delivering advice without offering any implementation support. 'Deliver results' is shorthand for real, hard-hitting, value-delivering activity.

To carry out this exercise, you need to keep one axis constant, otherwise the whole thing gets too complicated and unwieldy. So, let's say that the 'produce reports – deliver results' axis is constant. You are now in a position to identify various pairings for the vertical axis. We've put 'strategic versus tactical approach', but you can use the vertical to address any number of differentiators to do with products, services, capabilities, assets, people, or any other relevant point of difference.

Then use techniques such as research, workshops and brainstorming sessions to compile different charts, each with a different vertical axis. In each case, map your competitors, substitutes, and, of course, your own organization. When you overlay all of the completed charts you will get an immediate picture of where you have any real differentiation from your competitors or substitutes.

To sum it up...

You are not competing against your competitors' offerings. You are competing against their value propositions. Your value proposition needs to be compelling enough to be able to: overcome the value proposition of your competitors (taking care that you consider substitutes and all possible alternatives in your thinking, but manage to avoid 'analysis paralysis'!) and overcome the 'do-nothing' or 'in-house' options.

You also need to be able to prove your claims. In the next chapter we'll examine how you can substantiate your value.

Notes

1. The Five Competitive Forces that Shape Strategy, Michael Porter, *Harvard Business Review*, January 2008.
2. *Blue Ocean Strategy*, W. Chan Kim and Renée Mauborgne, Harvard Business School Press, 2005.
3. Creating new market space, W. Chan Kim and Renée Mauborgne, *Harvard Business Review*, Jan–Feb 1999.

10 Value Proposition Builder: Proof

A major reason for becoming a value-led organization is to win more business and grow your business profitably. A critical factor in this is being able to *prove* your value. Potential customers require evidence of your capability and value – in a world made cynical by hype, your word is simply not enough.

Therefore, the best way of providing a reason to choose you is through the provision of credible evidence to prove your claims. Show your results and associated performance data. A variety of tried and tested techniques are available to help you:

- case studies;
- write a book and become a thought leader;
- develop articles for use on- and off-line;
- publish customer testimonials;
- a value calculator.

This last point relates to the need to adopt formal measurement techniques to measure and track the impact of your value proposition – a value calculator. Several means are available to enable you to do this.

Where a product or service is sold on a transactional basis, it may be relatively easy to show the value of a sale by using straightforward formulas. For example: 'We have scientific evidence to show that our fertilizer produces 5 per cent better yield than our competitor's product. But the cost of our product, per hectare, is only 2 per cent higher than the competitor product.' However, more complex solutions (for example, information technology systems sales, or business process outsourcing deals) will require more substantial, detailed analysis – a key part of which is benefits realization.

Once upon a time, companies could set out their claimed benefits without much by way of proof. Today, that won't cut it. Claims must be detailed and substantiated. Here is a simple example.

'Although the set-up cost of our product/service is 12 per cent higher than the next best alternative, lower maintenance costs (which normally amount to 19 per cent of the set-up cost over five years of operation, compared to 37 per cent from the next best alternative) result in a five-year ownership cost that is 3.72 per cent cheaper, *plus* there is less downtime.'

	Our product	**Next best alternative**
Set-up cost	112.00	100.00
Maintenance for 5 years	19% = 21.28	37% = 37.00
Set-up + maintenance	133.28	137.00

What we are edging towards here is 'total cost of ownership', a measurement system frequently used by technology companies because the lifetime costs of a system can be significant multiples of the initial costs. So, total cost of ownership tools or spreadsheets are used to demonstrate to clients the true total cost of purchase over the purchase lifetime. This is often used as part of a return-on-investment calculation that may go into a building a business case for the purchase of the item or service.

Total cost of ownership (TCO), return on investment (ROI) and cost–benefit (C–B)

TCO, ROI and C–B are all types of business case analysis. Each term implies a different approach to the general business case question: 'What are the likely financial and other business consequences if we take this or that action (or decision)?' Whether developing your own case or evaluating someone else's, remember that none of these terms has a single precise or universally agreed definition. Therefore, it is important to document and communicate which cost (and/or benefit) line items are included (and which are not), the time period covered, and major assumptions used in calculating financial metrics. Here are some of the characteristics of each approach.

TCO

TCO is the total cost of a product or service (acquisition, installation, use, maintenance, modification and disposal) right across its useful life. Because all relevant aspects of operation are included, TCO is always more than the initial purchase price. In the case of many of the large purchases to which TCO is applied (for example, computer systems, power plants, defense systems) high multiples apply – maybe 10 or 20 times the initial purchase price.

It can be quite challenging to decide upon the right set of criteria to include in a TCO analysis. To be meaningful, a TCO analysis should be as comprehensive in its scope as possible, and must lend itself to line-by-line, 'apples-to-apples' comparisons with alternatives.

If a cost of ownership estimate is limited to the cost side of a cost–benefit analysis, and to just one possible operational scenario, it may be only a partial answer. There are advantages to the inclusion of benefits, and the use of different operational scenarios – for example, 'business as usual' versus 'change'.

Do bear in mind that a TCO analysis is limited. It is not designed to capture financial gains that may come from increased revenues, or increased business volume, or improved competitiveness, and so on. This means that TCO analysis alone is usually not sufficient to provide the basis for estimating return on investment, or payback period. On its own, TCO analysis is a basis for valid decision making when all possible actions differ only with respect to cost.

Case study using TCO

Let's take a look at an example of an organization – call it RealEng, a 3,500-person engineering consultancy with unpredictable growth – using total cost of ownership.

Here are some background facts about its data distribution and storage:

- 12 terabytes of data spread across 450 servers in various locations;
- 96 regional offices connected via WAN links ranging from 128kB to 100MB;
- 80 copies of backup and restore software driving an assortment of 172 autoloader and direct attached tape drives;
- tape off-siting solution by postal service (tapes are posted to central storage depot).

Some key issues related to these data requirements are:

- 70 per cent data growth.
- Backup failure rate running at 7 per cent.
- Tape drive capacity on larger servers is limited.
- Software management overhead.
- Service level target (not service level agreement) of 48 hours.
- The business lacks confidence in its ability to restore the data, should a problem arise.
- The backup window is being exceeded – if backups are still running when the business needs to be operational, then time and money are lost.
- There is a significant tape management overhead – tapes are all manually loaded, unloaded and packed for postage.
- There is an off-siting management overhead – unpacking, categorizing and storing tapes.
- Full backups at weekends are not possible owing to bandwidth constraints.

The proposed solution to these issues is a secure, remote, managed (SRM) backup and restore service. But how can the efficacy of a proposed solution be quantified? RealEng needs help with the business case because not all of the relevant data are to hand. With costs in so many different places, RealEng hasn't got an accurate measure of the current total costs. Hardware and software will account for only between 15 per cent and 25 per cent of the total costs, so to get a valid assessment of the proposed SRM solution, it is vital to quantify people costs, poor service costs, business risk and service level improvements.

Current: RealEng costs to meet Service Level Targets (SLT) with restores in 8 hours

Categories	Year 0	Year 1	Year 2	Year 3	Year 4	Year 5	Total
Depreciation Cost of Media Cost of Hardware Cost of Software Replacement costs							
Sub total	£308,237	£405,680	£548,836	£600,017	£802,177	£914,177	£3,270,886
Maintenance for break fix Media Hardware Software							
Sub total	£261,060	£269,200	£312,280	£374,740	£532,760	£877,600	£2,366,580
CAPEX Media Hardware Software							
Sub total	£22,210	£262,330	£961,550	£720,170	£624,810	£1,097,550	£3,666,410
Implementation Additional deployment Additional technology refresh							
Sub total	£4,500	£33,000	£244,500	£103,500	£294,000	£402,000	£1,077,000
Staff costs Management Recruitment							
Sub total	£400,000	£427,475	£602,910	£851,895	£913,278	£1,142,724	£3,938,281
Recovery costs	£215,500	£215,500	£280,500	£315,000	£424,250	£643,625	£1,878,875
Operational costs (post, etc) Tape strorage environment							

Postage &
courier, 2 sets
per week
Courier
– emergency
restores

Sub total	£58,480	£58,480	£65,880	£76,980	£93,630	£118,605	£413,575

Total direct costs of current backup environment	£1,269,987	£1,671,665	£3,016,445	£3,042,302	£3,684,904	£5,196,280	£16,611,607

New: Projected SRM backup and restore service pricing to Service Level Agreement with restores in 4 hours

Set up
Tele-
communications
Annual
operating costs
Transition costs

Total	£800,277	£955,235	£1,019,754	£1,220,679	£1,302,943	£1,401,113	£6,700,000

The total cost of the current backup and restore service over a 5 year period is £16,611,607.
The total cost of the proposed new SRM backup and restore solution over a 6 year period (the first year is set up and migration) is £6,700,000.

Difference: The total saving of switching to the new SRM solution over 5 years is £9,911,606.

On the basis of the TCO modelling, which was much more extensive than we can show here, RealEng decided to go with the SRM backup and restore solution.

The commercial benefits include:

- £9,911,606 saved over 5 years
- Disaster recovery enabled solution
- Predictable costs for the contract term
- Flexibility in terms of divestments
- Service level agreements (rather than service level targets) for restores, business continuance and disaster recovery
- Restores within 4 hours

ROI

ROI has several possible meanings, so, to start, there is the need to get clarity around which definition is being used. The financial sector uses ROI to mean return on invested capital, where an organization's total capital is divided into its EBITDA (a snappy initialism for 'earnings before interest, taxes, depreciation and amortization'). ROI is also used to mean return on assets, an organization's income for a period divided by the value of assets used to produce that income.

The simplest and most generally used definition, however, is incremental gain from an activity. So, if a $100 investment pays back $150, that is a 50 per cent ROI. The important point is to make sure that you understand the definition in use in any particular circumstance.

C–B

As the term suggests, C–B analysis weighs costs against benefits. Here again, it is important to establish the definitions of those terms (and what goes into each category) at the outset of any analysis.

A properly designed C–B analysis is quite a complex undertaking. Because it must permit colleagues to make valid judgements, and decisions, about a business case, it must include as many relevant factors (hard and soft) as possible, and show the timings of proposed inflows and outflows. Some of these elements can be hard to quantify: if, for example, a project is intended to deliver some sort of 'corporate image improvement', or 'improved workplace', how are those to be measured in monetary terms?

A key output from a C–B analysis is a time-based cash flow summary. This will serve as the basis for calculating such things as net and discounted cash flows, payback periods and more. If the cash flow statement also shows individual cost and benefit line items, it can serve as an effective tool for risk management and optimization of returns.

Summary

Providing evidence of your value is critical for your ongoing success. Deciding which measures to use and then implementing them and communicating the results will help enormously when it comes to growing sales and keeping your business focused on value.

11 Value proposition template and value proposition statement

Completing the VP template and creating your VP statement

We've now completed the Value Proposition Builder™ process. We've deconstructed and reconstructed the way an organization delivers value to its customers. So what does the final output look like?

By way of illustration, we set out in Tables 11.1 and 11.2 a simple value proposition (VP) template,[1] together with a hypothetical worked-up example for a corporate tax practice for a medium-sized accounting firm.

Once you have created your VP template, it then remains to summarize this into a value proposition statement. For our tax practice, their statement reads as follows:

> You are important to us and, through our partner-led approach, we work with you to ensure planning and tax compliance is fully integrated and operates effectively within the context of your business, enabling you to minimize risk, while delivering clarity and effectiveness in your tax philosophy.
>
> Our account management approach ensures one single partner has a comprehensive overview of the tax service delivery. This provides you

with a single point of contact, allowing you to achieve rapid decision making, solve problems and maximize efficiency.

Our prices remain competitively aligned with the value we deliver and are 10% less than the top global firms.

Table 11.1   Ten-point value proposition template

	Ten-point value proposition template	Corresponding areas in Figure 2.4	Functional Responsibility
1	Who is the intended customer?	Market	VP team with Board sponsor
2	What will the customer's experience be of the offering and the company, and what price will they pay?	Value experience	VP team with Board sponsor
3	What offerings will we create to deliver the intended experience to the intended customer? What purchase or usage of offerings do we want from the intended customer?	Offerings	VP team with Board sponsor
4	What benefits will the customer derive from the experience and at what cost?	Benefits	VP team with Board sponsor
5	What competing alternatives do the customers have? How are we different?	Alternatives & differentiation	VP team with Board sponsor
6	How will we substantiate our ability to deliver the resulting customer experience measurably and specifically?	Proof	VP team with Board sponsor
7	Over what time frame will the proposition be delivered to the customer?		VP team with Board sponsor
8	How will the value proposition be communicated internally and externally?		Marketing & sales
9	How will the value proposition be operationalized throughout the business?		Operations & HR
10	How will we measure and monitor the effectiveness of the proposition on our business?		Balanced scorecard and finance

Table 11.2   Value proposition template for tax practice

Value proposition template for tax practice	
1 Who is the intended customer?	Finance directors and tax directors of large, UK-based organizations who are looking for high-quality corporate tax advice at a price that is lower than the largest accounting firms
	We want to attract new corporate tax clients, a number of whom will be FTSE 250 companies
2 What will the customer's experience be of the offering and the company, and what price will they pay?	Our clients will receive a first-class tax service. This means that the key relationship partner from our firm will be in frequent and regular contact, as agreed with the client, and will have full transparency and awareness of the tax situation. All levels of staff working on the account will be fully briefed, trained and informed so that the client has confidence in our tax team and is enabled to make rapid decisions.
	Through building a seamless, transparent and strong consultative relationship between our firm and the client, the client will understand that they are paying the right amount of tax for their business, at minimized risk. The risk mitigation is achieved through full integration of tax planning and tax compliance, and first-class communications.
	Our prices are within the upper quartile but always competitively aligned with the value we deliver and less than the largest firms by at least 10%.

Table 11.2 *(Continued)*

Value proposition template for tax practice

| 3 | What offerings will we create to deliver the intended experience to the intended customer? What purchase or usage of offerings do we want from the intended customer? | We will ensure we have a core offering for all tax clients, extending into full handling of all elements of management and risk. |

Core tax offer
- Tax Accounting
- Computations & Returns
- Tax Payments
- Enquiries

Extended offer elements
Risk approach
- Strategic priorities/board profile
- Pre-audit planning
- Tax policy/philosophy
- Disclosure policy
- External regulation

Risk profile
- Regulatory environment
- Sector specialism
- IR assessment

Assurance
- Deadline management
- Proprietary software functionality
- Risk-based review of internal accounts systems
- Use IT to maximum, but balanced with personal interaction and commercial judgement
- Transparency

Issues focused
- Strategic priorities
- Board profile
- Sector specialism
- Internal system/control environment
- Internal/external audit requirements

Table 11.2   *(Continued)*

Value proposition template for tax practice	

	We would like all clients to choose to purchase a full range of tax offerings from us.
4 What benefits will the customer derive from the experience and at what cost?	**Benefits** • Clear and commercial tax advice and service • Open and effective communications leading to speed of operation • Minimized risk • Partner-led relationships that ensure confidence **Cost** • Higher price than smaller firms • Less 'halo' effect and 'clout' when compared with largest firms • Sometimes slower in turnaround than largest firms
5 What competing alternatives do the customers have? How are we different?	**Alternatives** • Use largest accounting firms • Recruit internal tax director and staff • Use several smaller firms to supply tax services **Differentiation** We are different because we can provide the quality of the largest firms at a lower price, with better efficiency, effectiveness and clarity than the range of smaller firms. Since our whole practice is working on a range of clients and problems, we can bring this fresh thinking to bear for the benefit of our clients – providing greater effectiveness than the internal alternative.

Table 11.2 *(Continued)*

Value proposition template for tax practice	
6 How will we substantiate our ability to deliver the resulting customer experience measurably and specifically?	Benefits realization programme Return on Investment analysis Creation of case studies and testimonials Writing thought leadership articles and white papers
7 Over what time frame will the proposition be delivered to the customer?	The core offer will run for the next five years Additional elements to the tax offering set will be created/refreshed every six to twelve months.
8 How will the value proposition be communicated internally and externally?	**Internal** • Management/internal opinion leader briefings • Value champions • Intranet & splash screens in major offices • Office promotions • E-mail bulletins • Print – posters, newsletters, stickers, Post-its, • SMS • Senior partner updates **External** • Value-based advertising • Sales presentations • Word-of-mouth promotion to clients • Interpersonal relationships • Press toolkit • Recruitment vehicles – university presentations, internet, ads, recruiters • Collateral material – brochures, flyers

Table 11.2   *(Continued)*

Value proposition template for tax practice	
9 How will the value proposition be operationalized throughout the business?	• 'Value champions' from each area of the tax practice, instilling and inculcating our new value processes and ethos within their business area • Training a core group of tax partners to deliver this kind of seamless tax service • Series of workshops and cascade programmes • Reorganization of the tax practice in certain key areas to ensure value alignment • Restructuring of management so that customers have a single partner responsible for the whole tax – ensuring value delivery • New reward programmes based on customer value experience
10 IIow will we measure and monitor the effectiveness of the proposition on our business?	Benefits realization programmes Balanced scorecard Management teams

The value proposition statement, remember, is not the boilerplate or elevator pitch for your firm and is never to be used externally. It is the articulation of your value upon which other messaging is developed. As we quoted in Chapter 2, Lanning[2] says:

A value proposition is:

- *about* customers but *for* your organization;
- not addressed to customers but must drive these communications;
- articulates the essence of a business, defining exactly what the organization fully intends to make happen in the customer's life.

In the following chapter we will examine how to deliver your value proposition, including how to develop and generate your internal messages and messages to market.

Intel, and an exercise in getting your head around value propositions

We have defined a value proposition statement as a clear, compelling and credible expression of the experience that a customer will receive from a supplier's measurably value-creating offer, where Value = Benefits minus Cost.[3] Now, the idea of an 'expression of an experience' may sound rather vague, but Intel is a perfect example to demonstrate the principle.

We probably all know of Intel. The company has, for 30 or more years, been a major force in our unfolding digital world: the world's leading innovator and manufacturer of microprocessors. Indeed, 'Intel Inside' is one of the most universally recognized and trusted advertising slogans. Through continuous innovation (this is a company that has, for decades, invested an average 15 per cent of revenue in research and development) Intel has achieved a dominant, respected position in its industry.

So here's a starter exercise for you... jot down what you think is the essence of Intel's top-level value proposition.

OK? Now let's start to analyse the issue.

What does the customer want?

A key challenge that Intel has faced, right from the outset, is that there is little point in asking end users what they want in terms of the technology, because they just don't know and, therefore, cannot say.

Since 2005, Intel has operated what it calls its Tick-Tock development model: every year, the company either Ticks or Tocks. When it Ticks, it scales down the size of the transistors; when it Tocks, it changes the micro-architecture of the chip. Thus 2008 was a Tock year, in which Intel introduced its new Nehalem architecture; while 2009 is a Tick year in which it scales down to a 32 nanometer manufacturing process. And 2010 is a Tock year when the architecture evolution leaps ahead and yet another new micro-architecture will be introduced (Figure 11.1). At this rate by 2020, Intel will be approaching the limits of Moore's Law,[4] so there'll have to be innovation of a different kind!

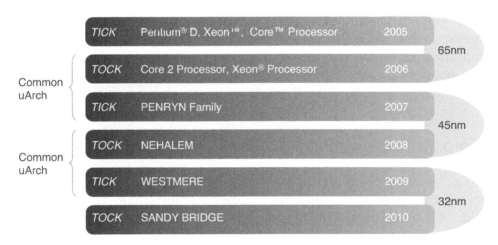

All dates, product descriptions, availability and plans are forecasts and subject to change without notice.

Figure 11.1   Intel's Tick-Tock model

However, the point is, asking end users to comment on, say, the Nehalem architecture, or Intel's Atom architecture, would not be productive, per se. Nor would it help to ask users if they want a 22-nanometre chip in 2012.

In fact, Intel's research shows that many of the companies who retail and resell the computers powered by Intel chips, and many end users themselves, do not welcome the fruits of all these endeavors. Why? Because they represent uncertainty and change.

John Woodget, Intel's global head of telecommunications operations, says:

> Our research shows that end users don't want their PCs to become obsolete. People are reluctant to change. And yet our whole industry is driving change. Our retail and resale customers don't like it because it's hard to manage the inventory part of it: it's very hard to change the products and the branding and the positioning. And end users don't like it because they'll learn one application and then, suddenly, something new is happening. As soon as you've got a more powerful processor – guess what? – software can take advantage of that and new applications emerge. The industry starts pushing products using these new applications. People find it hard to keep up with these changes.

This gives rise to an interesting insight. For intermediaries and end users, introducing the new fruits of Intel's brilliant technological labours goes on the cost side of the VP equation, not the benefits side. From a customer's perspective, the introduction of new technological marvels can be a pain as well as a bonus.

Chips with everything

To get at the Intel value proposition, it is counter-intuitively necessary to get away from the technological aspects of the situation – although it is, of course, paradoxically necessary for Intel to continue to meet its targeted technological advancements.

Doctor Scholasticus's philosophical question is answered. Ten thousand angels can dance on the head of a pin. And the mind of Busby Berkeley will be virtualized to do the choreography. X million circuits can be etched on a dollar chip. Or maybe it's Y million and ten cents. Pointless setting frontiers to your thought by speculated limitations on hardware. There aren't any. In 1950, the man who had kickstarted the computer age with a $1 million personal donation to the US Navy, IBM's chief Thomas J. Watson, estimated that his company, which was then really the only game in town, might be able to sell two or even three computers a year.

His thinking, atypically, was bounded by the 55-feet long, 8-feet wide Harvard Mark I computer he had funded in 1943 and its attendant army of acolytes. But Harvard had already been overtaken by Cambridge. The all-electronic computers spawned by ENIAC were a thousand times faster and down to mere two-car garage size. By the mid-1950s IBM was selling computers that would actually fit inside a room to scores of American companies and Watson was wiping egg off his face all the way to the bank.

Today, there are billions of personal and enterprise computers worldwide. And several million times the processing power, memory and storage space of the clattering, whirring Harvard giant rest negligently in the lap of any businessperson commuting the stratosphere between meeting and meeting.

But that, of course, is counting only computers that look like computers. The general purpose and specifically dedicated workhorses we know as computers, dazzlingly sophisticated as they now are and will increasingly become, are simply the residual bottom layer in an evolutionary process – the first move of a revolution that long ago proceeded much further, reaching into every corner of human life everywhere on earth, and everywhere off earth that human influence and ambition so far extend.

Now, in the same way as steam power and abundant iron coincided to put the world on rails, and internal combustion and the aerofoil mated to put it on wings, each development releasing massive and irreversible forces of social and commercial change, so the microprocessor is powering the converged digital world that is just now taking off.

Regardless of economic downturns and upturns, the microprocessor chip is the motive force of all the new technologies on which the world now turns and will turn. Ever more complex, more intricate, more densely packed with circuits. Ever more capable of ever more thought-defying tasks. Simultaneously, ever more miniaturized, so that the smallest examples seem in danger of shrinking till they disappear out of the universe altogether. Yet, conversely, ever cheaper and faster. These exquisitely tiny Fabergé eggs and Cellini jewels of technology are priced ever more competitively, rather like the cost of the pig iron that built the railways.

An appropriate comparison. The chip is a supremely sophisticated finished artefact. But it is the raw material of technology.

So, what's the value proposition?

Only connect

What all of this shows is that Intel's top-level value proposition, in general terms, has to do with capability, connectivity and collaboration – the ability to do things that would otherwise be impossible. Earlier chips made stand-alone capabilities possible. By enabling Web 2.0 and more, today's Intel chips enable the social and commercial connectedness that today's users expect.

It's worth noting here that the computer started life by more efficiently doing things that were done before (spreadsheets versus tabular balance sheets, word processing versus typewriting, e-mail versus mail), then it moved to doing things that could not have been done before, such as accessing information over the global internet and, more recently, enabling social networking, e-commerce and machine-to-machine interoperability. The benefits of learning to use these new tools and new ways of working outweigh the costs of upgrading and the challenges of constantly learning new ways. So, today's users are prepared to put up with the periodic costs of upgrading – both financial and in terms of learning new things.

It's a reality that applies as much to young people as older ones. John Woodget again:

> If you go out and ask customers what they want, they'll tell you they want stability, ease of use... things that we are not delivering. One of the surprising things is that that is as true for young people as old. We've done research into Gen Y[5] consumers: they do it [use technology] because it's socially required, not because they like new technology. There's a maturity dimension to the value proposition here. The original VP of the PC was being able to do some very specialist stand-alone applications. Then the internet came enabling networked things. Now, social networking is coming along and collaboration is increasingly important, and the next stage is people are beginning to want to use their mobile phone to do similar things.

I would add that in the longer term they will expect a seamless experience across all their internet devices, they will expect seamless continuity of data and services whether they take a photo with a camera or from a webcam, and they will expect it to be available to share on their and others' phones, PCs or TVs. They will expect it to become easy to talk and socialize using whatever device is convenient – in the kitchen or on a train.

So, the benefits that Intel empowers have to do with the experiential outcomes of being able to do exciting new things. But there are costs that include the price and the need to get familiar with the new software and other complications of the more advanced product.

Responding to customers' needs for social and collaborative connectivity at a manageable price, Intel is now working on another strand of innovation. John Woodget's remit is Intel's activities with the telecommunications (telco, in industry parlance) sector. As he sums it up:

> With the telcos, it's a whole different model. They really have far less interest in the technology, or managing the inventory, or worrying whether it's a particular brand. They're much more interested in delivering a user experience. But, they are also interested in winning subscribers, reducing churn, and maximizing average revenue per user (ARPU), and we have the Atom product that's changing our relationship with them because they've found that there's a complete device, called a Netbook, with which they can bundle broadband connectivity, and win subscribers.
>
> In 2007, Asus brought out a Netbook – the Eee PC – tiny keyboard, an 8-inch screen – and the category as it's now being defined is a 10-inch screen, which is just about the size for a reasonable keyboard. They're pretty good devices as a companion to a PC, great for connectivity. Telcos love this because it's an always-connected device. They like it because it's mobile, and it's cheap, so they can use a subsidy model to win customers. But for us it's interesting because there's a risk that it commoditizes the PC. There's a risk that they sell these things instead of a Notebook, which is a very capable device, and end users might be disappointed. So we're doing a lot of work at the moment about the value propositions: you know, what is good? What is better? What is best? And, of course, it depends on the usage model. For me, it's fascinating because, for Intel, the consumer is reached through Original Equipment Manufacturers (OEMs) and retail, but now, suddenly, telcos could be a material segment of our business in the next three to five years, with a totally different financial model that we don't fully understand. And the VP that they're working with their customers is very different from the value proposition of a retailer to a transactional customer. So the whole VP thing assumes that the OEMs and the retailers look after our

customers for us, and we know that our job is to innovate products...
but the innovation of the product platform has always been a static
application or an internet-application platform. As we move into the
mobile internet device world, it's not only about applications but also
services. These are very exciting times.

Do you want to change your mind about Intel's top-level value
proposition?

(Our version of the Intel value proposition is given in Appendix B.)

When John Woodget talks about the research Intel has done into
Gen Y consumers and their expectations of a seamless experience
across all their internet devices, we liken this to a good example of
how Intel have 'crossed the chasm'.[6] Intel needs to convince both the
early and late majority to buy their products (see Chapter 7).

How has it done this? By focusing on the full user value experience
and ultimately the value proposition, not the technology. What Intel
is offering is not the power or speed of its chips but what can be
experienced through having its chips in a variety of devices. Gen Y
want seamless collaboration so that's what they'll get.

Timelines

How long does all this take? As always, that's like asking 'How long is a
piece of string?' and is dependent upon how aligned your organization
is, how committed your senior executives are, how cynical and tired
your organization is about new initiatives or, indeed, whether you
have initiative overload, and all the other similar factors you need to
take into consideration. See our comments in Chapter 14 on assessing

Activity Week commencing	Wk 1	Wk 2	Wk 3	Wk 4	Wk 5	Wk 6	Wk 7	Wk 8	Wk 9	Wk 10	Wk 11	Wk 12
Identify & document internal activities, priorities and beliefs	→→											
Undertake market and customer analysis		→→→→→→→→→→→→										
Research value experience with customers			→→→→→→→→→→→→									
Analyse and map your offerings			→→→→→→→→→→→→→→→→									
Map your benefits										→→		
Analyse the alternatives available to your customers and understand your differentiation							→→→→→→→→					
Create evidence and proof of how you deliver your value						→→→→→→→→→→→→						
Analyse conclusions with stakeholders and set direction											→	
Develop 12–18 month implementation plan												→

Figure 11.2 Timeline for value proposition building process

whether the conditions are right within your organization to start this process.

However, taking a view that you have everything listed previously sorted out, then a realistic and achievable timescale is shown in Figure 11.2.

Notes

1. Modified from *Delivering Profitable Value*, Michael J. Lanning, Perseus Publishing, 1998.
2. *Delivering Profitable Value*, Michael J. Lanning, Perseus Publishing, 1998.
3. Parallel with 'Carter's law' – Dennis Carter created the Intel Inside brand; his mantra was Satisfaction = Reality – Expectations. The brand promise sets an expectation and the purchase of a PC is the material instantiation of setting an expectation – very closely related to cost – while reality is the perceived benefit, and sure enough satisfaction is related to value.

4. This is the prediction that the number of transistors (hence the processing power) that can be squeezed onto a silicon chip of a given size will double every 18 months. Stated by Gordon Moore (a co-founder of Intel and its former chairman) in 1965, it has proven to be amazingly accurate over the years.

5. Generation Y, sometimes referred to as 'Millennials' or 'Net Generation', whose birth years range anywhere from the second half of the 1970s to around the year 2000, depending on the source, grew up in the 1990s and 2000s.

6. *Crossing The Chasm*, Geoffrey A. Moore, HarperCollins, 1991.

12 Message development

You may remember from Chapter 1 the response given at a conference when senior sales professionals were asked to define a value proposition, one said (to much laughter and applause): 'It's marketing bullshit for a benefits statement.' Well, sorry to disappoint, but no. Not even close.

For value-based messaging, all messages must spring from a common truth, the value your organization brings, and if you've followed the Value Proposition Builder™ process or value proposition process (VPP) described in the previous chapters you'll know that value proposition messages including statements are the output of this VPP. Naturally, you will want to communicate your value to the outside world but the core of the message will be based on the customer value experience and will have been drawn into being via rigorous questioning, filtering and sifting. Now you can't call that marketing bull.

In the Value Proposition Builder™ process, at the benefits stage you will have created a benefits map. This is the foundation for your value-based message development: the elements that are important, interesting and valued from a customer experience perspective. This is the start point for your message development.

Don't throw your money away

Before you start the message development, however, you need to decide on the purpose, direction and objective that your messaging is intended to meet. Messages cannot be created in isolation: there is no point. This is often how thousands of dollars, sometimes millions of dollars, get wasted every year by organizations asking marketing agencies[1] to develop messages for them. These messages, maybe for advertising, maybe for sales copy or product descriptors, then get created in isolation without going through a strategic, sometimes difficult process, such as the VPP. But the failure to create your messaging from your strategy down will result in messaging with no resonance and messaging that won't stand the test of time. So this is a shortsighted approach that will waste your money. We liken it to applying a Band-Aid or plaster to fix a broken leg!

So, you must first decide what you want to achieve. Clarity around your offerings? Increased awareness at the corporate level? Increased customer familiarity with a new set of services? Mobilization of your own organization around a common message set?

Once you have fixed your objective, you are ready to compile the value-based benefits that will resonate with your intended audiences.

Augmented benefits

As we determined in the Benefits chapter, the most valuable messages do not come from the expected benefits zone. They are, by and large, 'tickets to the game' – which is to say, they are absolutely necessary, but do not serve to differentiate your organization in any way. As an example, if a corporate law firm claims that it has qualified, experienced lawyers on its staff, any prospective client is likely to say 'So what?' because a corporate law firm without qualified, experienced lawyers can hardly call itself a corporate law firm! The valuable inputs from a messaging development standpoint are those in the augmented benefits zone (and, of course, in the potential benefits zone if some have emerged).

So, from your benefits map, select the augmented benefits zone. But, in order for these benefits to become usable as messages further refinement is necessary in order to establish that what you have is truly, repeatably valuable to your customers:

- You must analyse your competitors' messages and competing alternatives against the benefits statements that have been drawn out of the augmented benefits zone.
- You must refine your augmented benefits, ensuring you're not just duplicating messages from competitors.

Once these steps are done, you are in a position to create a message framework and hierarchy.

Creating a message framework and hierarchy

A three-step process will create high-impact, value-based messages that can be utilized by sales, marketing and internal communications departments:

1. Prioritize your value messages.
2. Identify the emotional, political and rational considerations of your customers to create message layers.
3. Draw together the messages, offers, and customer buyers to create focus.

Prioritize the value messages

Even the augmented benefits statements mapped via the benefits map may be in danger of becoming non-differentiated and thus not getting the attention they deserve. So, to create impact, prioritization and focus use a simple two-by-two matrix where the axes are 'client value' and 'competitive differentiation' (see Figure 12.1). Do the following:

-   Take each augmented (and, if available, potential) benefits statement.
-   Determine how *differentiated* it is from your competitors' or other alternatives.
-   Analyse how *valuable* it is to your customer.

The benefits that really count – the ones that have most weight and resonance with your intended audience – are those that represent a high degree of difference from your competitors' or alternatives, and represent high value for your customers. That's the top right-hand quadrant. These are high-impact messages. And the further up towards the top right-hand corner, the greater the 'Wow!' By contrast, messages that turn out to be in the lower left-hand quadrant are the least differentiating, and more likely to attract the 'So what?' dismissal.

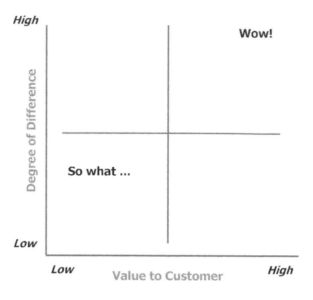

Figure 12.1   Prioritizing messages

That said, it is important to keep in mind that those statements that don't make the top right-hand quadrant are not to be dismissed because communication messages are layered and these can be utilized for the right target audience.

Categorize by message type

All messages are not created equal. They come in three flavours: rational, political and emotional (Figure 12.2). These three need to be considered in any communication (particularly those with prospects and customers) because they influence how people perceive value, and how they make decisions:

- Rational messages appeal to the logical needs of the recipient – matters of fact, content and detailing.
- Political messages respond to a recipient's organizational constraints and political issues.
- Emotional messages relate to gut feeling and instinct coupled with interpersonal relationships and the answers to the 'What's in it for me?' questions.

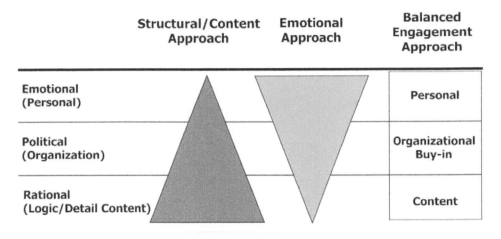

	Structural/Content Approach	Emotional Approach	Balanced Engagement Approach
Emotional (Personal)			Personal
Political (Organization)			Organizational Buy-in
Rational (Logic/Detail Content)			Content

Figure 12.2 All three layers of rational, political and emotional must be covered by your messaging

Communications that work take account of all three strands. This is where all of the things we have introduced start to come together in a co-ordinated manner to create powerful value-based communications.

Bring back to mind The Value Pyramid™ made up of four layers that depict the different types of 'units of sale', from component at the base to co-created value at the apex. As outlined earlier, selling components normally implies *transactional selling*, typically selling high volumes of lower-priced items via expert buyers (category procurement experts). By contrast, selling co-created value requires *consultative selling*, typically selling high-price ticket solutions on a one-to-one, or one-to-few, basis via expert influencers.

An expert influencer is someone who is expert in something, but not necessarily in some or all of the solution in question: for example, a chief sales officer (CSO) may know all there is to know about the sales goals and requirements of their organization, but when a customer relations management (CRM) solution is under discussion, she requires help to understand and decide on the technical aspects of the options open to her.

As these examples suggest, buyers at the component layer of the value pyramid are expert, but tend to be at lower levels in their organizational hierarchies than the senior people who have, of necessity, to be involved in the complex, high-price offers at the solutions and co-created value layers.

Using real client examples in Figure 12.3 we are actually able to show the degree of importance of rational, political and emotional messaging at each of the four layers of the value pyramid.

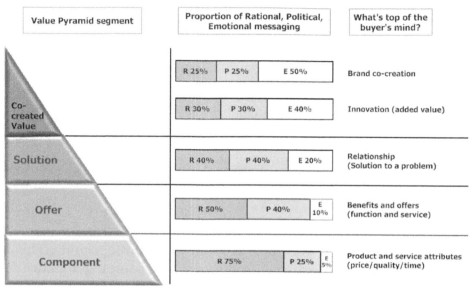

Key: R - Rational / P - Political / E - Emotional

Figure 12.3 The proportions of rational, political and emotional messaging suggested at each layer of The Value Pyramid™

Draw it all together

Armed with knowledge about your value messages (particularly those with a high degree of 'Wow!'), and the most valued offers in your portfolio, and the blend of rational, political and emotional considerations of your customers, you are in a position to draw everything together to create a focused message ladder. This can be overlaid onto The Value Pyramid™.

The example in Figure 12.4 is for a market research company.

Next, because you now understand the specific messages that resonate with specific audiences, you are able to allocate the messages to specific communications channels (Figure 12.4). Compile the messages onto one message matrix that includes the most appropriate communication channels for the respective audience types (Table 12.1).

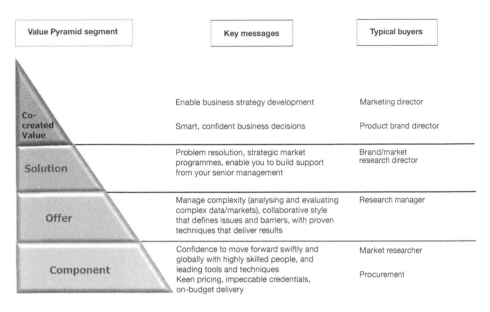

Value Pyramid segment	Key messages	Typical buyers
Co-created Value	Enable business strategy development	Marketing director
	Smart, confident business decisions	Product brand director
Solution	Problem resolution, strategic market programmes, enable you to build support from your senior management	Brand/market research director
Offer	Manage complexity (analysing and evaluating complex data/markets), collaborative style that defines issues and barriers, with proven techniques that deliver results	Research manager
Component	Confidence to move forward swiftly and globally with highly skilled people, and leading tools and techniques Keen pricing, impeccable credentials, on-budget delivery	Market researcher Procurement

Figure 12.4 Overlaying messages to target audiences onto The Value Pyramid™

Summary

Using genuine customer value experience, you will have refined, focused and made sure that all of your communications are tightly focused on your audiences. Importantly, these messages form the core of messages that come from your internal communications teams and both your marketing and sales teams – no more squabbling. Everyone is pointing towards customer value. That has to be good for business.

Note

1. The blame here doesn't lie with the marketing agencies; they are just doing what they're asked. The fault is with the commissioning organization for not owning and managing the project at a strategic level.

Table 12.1 Message matrix

Communications channel	Audience and Value Pyramid™ layer	Emotional messages	Rational messages	Political messages
Website **One-to-one targeting (via charity events, speaking opportunities etc.)** **Top-level account management**	**Co-created value** Marketing director	Working with you Exploring key issues Contributing extensive market & product insights	Understanding needs Developing appropriate hypotheses and testing them	
Website **Global PR surveys** **Thought leadership articles** **Centers of excellence**	**Co-created value** Product brand director	Helping you make smart, confident business decisions for your product brand	Quantitative and qualitative intelligence that delivers ongoing value	
Website **PR** **Speaking opportunities** **Thought leadership articles**	**Solutions** Brand/market research director	Working to understand your challenges, uncover underlying issues and develop projects to resolve	Develop market strategy programmes to create market positioning. Win–win results.	Providing a business plan and feasibility studies that enable you to build and win support from senior management

	Offers / Components			
Targeted events via account managers	**Offers** Market research director	Swiftly gain good understanding of requirements, define issues and barriers, work smoothly and collaboratively	Leading modelling techniques and tools, evaluate complex data/ markets to move product to launch	Proven established techniques, guaranteed to give excellent results in which you feel confident
Collateral material				
Sector white papers				
Breakfast briefings				
Search engine optimization				
Google PPC campaigns	**Components** Market researcher	Quickly pick up brief, establish issues, move project forward swiftly and safely	Our people are highly skilled, with leading tools, techniques, methodologies, etc.	Meet requirements, keep to deadlines, within budget, hit target
Online resource centre				
Newsletters				
Case studies				
Credentials				
How to... guides	**Components** Procurement	Established, safe, high-quality research house. Strong track record with impeccable credentials	Always meets specifics of Request for Proposal (RFP), complete documentation on time and in full, transparent pricing and project plans	Keenly priced for advanced modelling techniques used and capabilities deployed
Proposal documents				
Service sheets				

13 Implementation

Don't sell to customers, instead improve their value (delivery) systems.

(Michael J. Lanning)

Doing all of the things that we have described in this book will give you a powerful value toolset: a value proposition template (which, itself, clarifies your market focus, value experience, offerings, benefits, alternatives and differentiation, and supporting proof) and a value proposition statement. In addition, as you implement the steps necessary to create a value-focused enterprise (that is, addressing your strategic intent, business model, operating model and operational practices, all from a value-centred standpoint) within which to use all of these tools, you will more and more experience the cohesion, alignment and great results that value focus delivers.

Which brings us to the issue of the ways in which you apply and implement your value proposition. Here, we focus on three areas of implementation:

1. Alignment of value: to customers, with your people, with suppliers, and channel partners.
2. Sales and marketing tools: how to help sales and marketing people create value, sales opportunity and qualification tools, offering management.
3. Ideas for new strategic marketing tools.

So we begin with alignment of value.

Four constituencies, one goal – alignment of value

Customers, your people, suppliers and channel partners are four key constituencies of your enterprise. The key question, and big question, at this stage is: 'How can our value experience best be delivered, in a manner that engages all of the available enthusiasm, intelligence and energy of all stakeholders and is fully aligned with our value proposition?'

The answer is to stop treating our organization as a 'closed system' and start treating it as an 'extended enterprise'. Rather than 'doing things to' people (employees, suppliers, customers and, even, in some cases, competitors) you 'do things with' them.

So, the next question is: 'What do you need to do to make your organization this kind of dynamic, collaborative, aligned entity that will spontaneously attract all of the enthusiasm, intelligence and energy of all parties?' Well, there are several obvious answers that include:

- information systems;
- channel partners and strategic alliances;
- co-creative teams;
- individual relationships.

Let's look at each of these.

Information systems

- Ensure that all information systems and information technology (IS/IT) puts the customer first.
- If this is to work across all touchpoints (suppliers, etc) it must mean that the IS/IT is integrated with the value proposition (VP) – supply, distribution, sourcing must all be congruent with the VP.
- To address delivery as a 'cross-stakeholder' value package, it is vital to measure value, not just cost, because all stakeholders are involved.
- Everybody must be connected – every stakeholder must be able to enter into the collaborative milieu.

- There is the need to enable decision making as near to the customer as possible (particularly perhaps in selling situations).
- Information must always be 'action-enabling'. This means avoiding information overload, and adding value at every transfer point.

Channel partners and strategic alliances

- Partners and strategic alliances with all stakeholders need to be three-dimensional: strategy, cultural fit, operations.
- There is a need to understand strengths, weaknesses and boundaries.
- Put champions in place.
- Transfer learning continuously.
- Enable rapid change capability to follow changing economic, political and market forces.

Co-creative teams

- Because, in a value-creating environment, co-creative teams include not just employees, but also customers, suppliers and others, there is a need to recognize that there will, from time to time, be breakdowns between constituencies.
- There is the need, therefore, to understand and manage 'the power of compatible differences'.
- There is the need for different constituencies to build trust, and often thrive on ambiguity.

Individual relationships

- The value-focused enterprise must be based upon an alignment of strategic intent, the power of compatible differences, and shared commitments to results.
- This explicitly requires a very high level of trust between all parties – and trust is essential for speed of decision making, elimination of duplication and non-value-add, and turning breakdowns into breakthroughs.
- This means, inevitably, the need for strong organizational support, not least selecting first-class champions to lead the change.

Alignment across the entire organization is always going to be tricky.

'It's one thing for decision makers to understand customer experience but communicating it across the organization is another thing entirely. Organizations need to work smart and hard to get the message across in a way that is meaningful to staff in their day-to-day jobs,' says Ann Sinclair, head of the Customer Experience Program at Fujitsu. 'When senior executives do not regularly interact with their customers they don't get a realistic view of whether the quality of customer interactions is genuinely improving. And they don't see and experience for themselves the challenges their staff face every day', she says.

Suppliers

In many organizations, suppliers are relatively neglected – treated like second-class citizens. If you encourage someone to feel second class, that's the way they'll perform. And yet, in today's business environment, you need to engender a sense of collective ownership. You need suppliers to work enthusiastically with you rather than for you. And that can really only happen if your suppliers understand your strategic goals and are aligned with your organization.

It is a cliché to observe that we all now live in a networked world and that the interconnectivity enables the hypercompetitive environment in which we all operate, where competitors can appear, from anywhere, at any time. What sometimes gets sidelined is the fact that the very same connectivity enables organizations of all kinds and sizes to network seamlessly with their suppliers.

Advanced forms of this are demonstrated by some of the business process outsourcing deals that now provide a vast range of high-quality services at lower cost than host companies could otherwise achieve, and by collaborative innovation methodologies such as Procter & Gamble's startlingly clever Connect + Deliver programme.

An important aspect of getting 'Value' (with a capital V) from supplier relationships has to do with an alignment of 'values' (with a lower case v). Value (Benefits minus Cost) and values (the set of beliefs that guide an organization's behaviour) need to come from the same source, sing from the same song sheet, dance to the same tune. Relationships endure when there is an alignment of these 'hard' goals and 'soft' goals. David Maister says that individuals and organizations cannot excel in their performance unless they are prepared to act in accordance with an agreed set of principles, values and ideologies. He called this 'Values in Action:' the willingness to be accountable for progress towards goals, and to accept consequences for non-compliance.[1]

Your value proposition template is a great tool for checking this alignment with suppliers. Indeed, both value alignment and values alignment are increasingly important. One aspect of this was demonstrated in a paper from the Wharton School of the University of Pennsylvania,[2] in which marketing professor Barbara Khan made the point that: 'Research shows that in a competitive market, the perception that a company is socially responsible can be a major differentiation point for consumers, but it must be a sincere, deeply held element of the corporation's culture.'

If your 'values' are reflected in your value proposition (as they must be because your 'values' will influence your choices and approach to markets and offerings), the value proposition template that you produce can be used as a supplier reference check.

Innovative forms of networked enterprise:

Josiah Wedgwood

In the mid-18th century, Josiah Wedgwood was recognized as a great potter, but had a logistics problem: the growth of his business could only progress at the speed of a horse-drawn cart on a rutted road. Wedgwood saw that the only way to increase his business was by radical transport innovation. So, with the Earl of Bridgewater, he built one of Britain's earliest canals. Which, because it was an open transport system, fuelled the Industrial Revolution.

Star Alliance

In 1997, Air Canada, Lufthansa, SAS, Thai Airways International and United Airlines formed an alliance to provide seamless connectivity for their customers. This was a coming together of companies that, in various circumstances, were in competition with one another. But they sidelined any potential conflicts for the greater goal of satisfying their customers' travel needs in the best possible way. These kinds of arrangement gave rise to the term 'co-opetition'. Today, a significant number of competitors work together in different permutations of extended enterprises to serve customer needs. Organizational alignment to better satisfy customer wants and needs now takes many forms, and it is important to keep a very open mind about what is in the realm of the possible in order to deliver a customer value proposition.

Procter & Gamble Connect + Develop

The following is direct from the Connect + Develop website:

It's our version of open innovation: the practice of accessing externally developed intellectual property in your own business and allowing your internally developed assets and know-how to be used by others.

Historically, P&G relied on internal capabilities and those of a network of trusted suppliers to invent, develop and deliver new products and services to the market. We did not actively seek to connect with potential external partners. Similarly, the P&G products, technologies and know-how we developed were used almost solely for the manufacture and sale of P&G's core products. Beyond this, we seldom licensed them to other companies. Times have changed, and the world is more connected. In the areas in which we do business, there are millions of scientists, engineers and other companies globally. Why not collaborate with them? We now embrace open innovation, and we call our approach 'Connect + Develop'.

Today, open innovation at P&G works both ways – inbound and outbound – and encompasses everything from trademarks to packaging, marketing models to engineering, and business services to design. It's so much more than technology.

Our Innovation Needs:

On the inbound side, we are aggressively looking for solutions for our needs, but we also will consider any innovation – packaging, design, marketing models, research methods, engineering, technology, etc. – that would improve our products and services and the lives of the world's consumers. We have a lot to offer you as a business partner, and believe that together, we can create more value than we ever could alone.

P&G's Connect + Develop strategy already has resulted in more than 1,000 active agreements. Types of innovations vary widely, as do the sources and business models. Inbound or out, know-how or new products, examples of our success are as diverse as our product categories. We are interested in all types of high-quality, on-strategy business partners, from individual inventors or entrepreneurs to smaller companies and those listed in the FORTUNE 500 – even competitors.

What does it all mean for sales and marketing?

The organic growth of your organization self-evidently puts the spotlight on the two revenue-responsible functions of marketing and sales. So how does value proposition thinking operate here?

The question is particularly interesting because there is a great deal of evidence that, particularly in service- and solutions-selling business-to-business (B2B) enterprises, these two departments aren't always on the best of terms. In fact, they are often in a state of outright aggression. Why? Because they operate according to completely different goals: different objectives, different timescales, different budgets, different reward mechanisms.

The outcome, often, is that the sales team thinks that the marketing team are a bunch of effete so-and-sos who spend fortunes on 'creative' stuff that they 'throw over the wall' at sales, but it proves to be useless; and the marketing team thinks that the sales team are a bunch of oafs who have no appreciation of what they do.

Drawing on evidence from various sources, the picture of what is going on out there seems to be as follows.

Selling costs

Average sales costs of generating revenue are at an all-time high, and rising. Companies are spending increasing amounts to train sales people, and on sales assets.

Sales people and tools

Sales teams and individuals complain that they do not have the tools to be successful, and create 'clandestine collateral' to compensate. Sales people are conducting non-strategic or inappropriate activity. There is, perhaps unsurprisingly, a very high turnover of salespeople.

Interfunctional issues

As already indicated, sales and marketing departments work at cross-purposes, each blaming the other for failures. It is not a happy picture and the obvious question is, 'How can the situation be improved?' An excellent overview of the issue and solutions has been written by renowned academics Philip Kotler, Neil Rackham and Suj Krishnaswamy[3] but, here, we focus specifically on the development of value propositions for sales opportunities.

As overviewed earlier, sales tend now to be polarized as transactional or consultative, each of which has different strategies and economics. In consultative selling scenarios, the general 20th-century value proposition of 'a little extra value for a modestly higher margin' no longer works. The only way to win in a consultative scenario is to separate out and differentiate everything, including the sales force.

Transactional and consultative sales forces, processes and tools don't mix. Consultative sales people are too talented and expensive; they are overkill in a transactional sale. But if salespeople are given the two models to sell, they'll tend to default to transactional because it is the faster and in many respects easier option.

Marketing has been slow to understand this change and its implications. The fact is traditional marketing support tools do not work in the consultative sale. Which, in turn, asks the question: 'What is the role of marketing in the consultative sale, where solutions are highly customized and are developed during the sale?' The answers are: a) selecting the right opportunities, and b) creating tools to help sales people add value (see Figure 13.1).

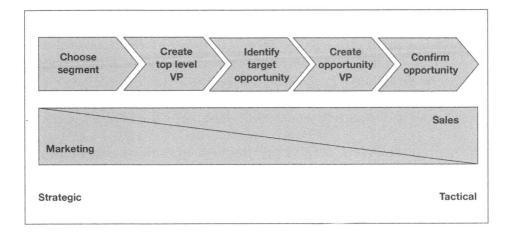

Figure 13.1 How marketing and sales work together in consultative selling

Tools to help sales people create value

It's always tempting to think of sales only from our own perspective, as a selling cycle. However, to understand the consultative sale (which is different in virtually every respect from the transactional sale) it is necessary to think in terms of the buying cycle – the way that whole process is and appears from the buyer's perspective.

It is a feature of the value-focused enterprise that all of its people are able to 'walk in the customer's shoes'. And, if you think about it, to walk in someone else's shoes, you first have to take off your own shoes. You really have to walk in the customer's shoes, look through the customer's eyes and think through the customer's mind. Only then will you be able truly to grasp the issues that are of concern to your prospective customer, and create an offering that will meet their needs and those of your own organization.

Times have changed quickly for us and selling has changed too. The issue for selling particularly in a downturn is not about discounting and lowering your price but is about continuing to add value and lowering the risk for your purchasers.

We have analysed what has changed in selling over 2008, and concluded that sales cycles are taking up to 40 per cent longer due to budget freezes and customers' decision processes taking longer. We have found that:

- Each potential purchase decision is scrutinized much more closely to analyse if they really do need to purchase now or if the decision can be delayed.
- More people are involved in the decision-making process and more sign-offs are required, which again lengthens the process.

The natural knee-jerk reaction to this is to just fill the sales funnel with more opportunities – 'surely something will drop'. No. Focus and stripping out the volume of opportunities to enable your teams to give more quality focus to less opportunity is the way to go. Better still that you nurture existing relationships, ideally where you are already trusted.

Before you sell anything, you must create value during the selling process itself. How do you do this? Ask yourself what things you can do for the customer that would provide so much value that the customer would pay for the sales meeting.

A good place to start is to focus on your customer's buying process – not on your own selling process. Once you have established your top level down to sale opportunity value proposition, then start to look at ways to enrich your relationship with your customer or prospect.

Below is a typical buying process; the full diagram for this is shown in Chapter 3, figure 3.6.

Recognition of need

That is, not the need for the buyer to become aware of your offering, but the need for the buyer to become aware of the need to which your offering relates and responds. (Traditional terms used for this stage include 'awareness' and 'interest'.)

What can you do to uncover customer needs? You must provide insights that make your customer's business better than it was already. Help them to identify an unrecognized problem or solution – something over and above what they thought the problem was and what they needed. Already you are adding value through your knowledge and insight. The earlier you can start creative solution shaping, the better the final result will be for you.

Depending upon what you're selling, you can do this through careful questioning, or you can provide problem analysis tools. These tools can be computer models or online tools that either you facilitate or the customer can use to self-diagnose. Even in high-end, consultative selling, you can provide self-diagnostic tools for the first part of this stage, followed by careful questioning when you are face to face with the customer. The first will strengthen and support the latter.

Evaluation of options

By now the buyer knows they have a need and they are looking at alternatives. As discussed under 'alternatives and differentiation', there is always the opportunity for an organization to react to a recognized need in a variety of ways. And, again as outlined earlier, two of the most popular choices are always the 'do-nothing' and 'in-house' options. So you have to convince a lead not to choose these options, nor to choose competitors' offerings and substitutes. But you will not do this by avoiding the issue: a buyer needs genuinely to go through the analytical processes necessary to review all options before proceeding. To win through, the important thing is that your value proposition outcompetes the other options. (Traditional terms used for this stage include 'viability', 'justification' and 'comparison'.)

Here you need to provide differentiation tools. You need to demonstrate what value you offer over and above the competition and over and above the buyer doing it themselves or doing nothing.

Resolution of concerns

If you have travelled this far with your prospect, you need next to put their mind at ease about the risks inherent in doing a deal with you. Is your value proposition sound from the buyer's perspective? What are the risks of selecting your company versus the other options? What if you fail to deliver as promised? Might it be politically safer for the buyer to choose the global player rather than your relatively small outfit? (Traditional terms used for this stage include 'selection' and 'conditional acceptance'.)

The old sales thinking about this phase in the process used to be about training your sales staff to be good at objection-handling. Frankly, it's a bit late in the day to be handling objections and if this is happening now, you probably haven't really got the commitment from your buyer to proceed anyway.

You need to be offering risk-reduction tools – ways that your customers can see that you are reducing the purchasing risk for them. Especially in consultative selling where you are co-creating a solution together with the purchaser, why wouldn't you offer to share the risk? You can share risk through pricing and how you construct the commercial terms of how you get paid. You can also share risk through offering a guarantee. You should also have clear credentials around where you have been successful elsewhere.

However, the ultimate way of de-risking the purchase for the buyer is to have an established relationship with the seller. In other words, trust is there. Trust allows people to buy freely from you again and again.

Once buyers have reached this stage, it's not uncommon for them to alternate backwards and forwards between the evaluation of options stage and the resolution of concerns stage. During these two stages, information about your organization becomes much more important. Here's what purchasers look for during these two stages to help them make the final 'yes' decision:

1. Up-to-date material. Complete and current information, including recent press releases about your company's successes.
2. Customers. Who else do you work with and what testimonials do you have?
3. History. What are your company's roots and its growth pattern?
4. Location(s). Do you have an office nearby? For some companies, especially manufacturers, it's a real plus to have a physical location in the vicinity even in the Internet Age.
5. Board of directors/advisors. Who are they? Successful and prominent directors can validate a company, especially in its growth years.
6. Media coverage. High-profile articles or a mass of media coverage can put you on the map.
7. Thought leadership. White Papers, blogs, etc offer an insight into the thinking and experience of a company's executives.

Settling terms

The end of the buyer's process is the negotiation and settling of terms. This is where your homework on, for example, total cost of ownership will come into its own. (Traditional terms used for this stage include 'business principles', 'final negotiation' and 'contract signing'.)

When you are involved in consultative selling and you step into the customer's shoes and appreciate the buying cycle, you will see that many traditional sales tools (for example, 'classic' glossy product brochures and sales presenters) are at best irrelevant, and at worst can be downright damaging. This is the source of many of the sales department's complaints about the marketing department's creation of collateral that gets thrown over the wall at them.

In the consultative sale, sales tools need to be tailored to the specific stages of the buying process. They must be customer focused and value creating. If, for example, you are at the 'recognition of need' stage, introducing the BRAIN offer that was outlined earlier (Chapter 2), there is the need to use research findings and thought leadership tools to help the prospective buyer understand the need and value of this kind of solution. Going in at this stage with a product-focused glossy brochure that lovingly describes every feature and flavour, every bell and whistle, of the offer ('the object-oriented taxonomic system is a world first') will likely, and rightly, get you shown the door.

Once you appreciate the very different circumstances and dynamics of the consultative sale and all that it entails, you will realize that there is a profound effect on the most central, the most expensive, the most important element of the sales process – the sales person.

Consultative sales are all about relationships built on intelligence, empathy and deep commitment to the creation of value for both the customer and the selling organization. Let's look briefly at the people issues.

People

At risk of stating the blindingly obvious, it is essential to make sure that your sales people have the appropriate behaviours and right skills and that they deliver profitable sales growth over the long term. But how is that best achieved?

In value selling, it is not sufficient, these days, just to focus on developing the sales skills of the people who do your selling. Instead, the most

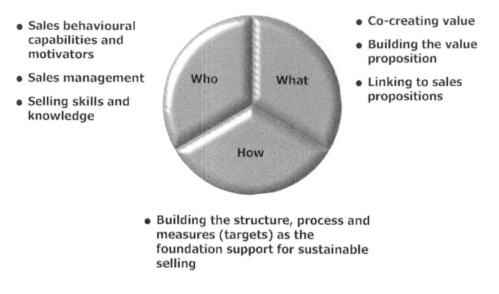

- Sales behavioural capabilities and motivators
- Sales management
- Selling skills and knowledge

- Co-creating value
- Building the value proposition
- Linking to sales propositions

- Building the structure, process and measures (targets) as the foundation support for sustainable selling

Figure 13.2   Creating sustainable sales

successful organizations blend three ingredients in equal proportions to achieve superior, sustainable sales performance (Figure 13.2):

- The behavior of their people – the 'who'.
- The processes and structures that underpin the organization and the sales team – the 'how'.
- The value proposition – the 'what'.

Any disconnect between these three ingredients in business development will undermine performance and impact sales and revenue. Consequently, it is vital to understand the underlying elements that make up each component and how they impact your sales operation and, more importantly, how well or otherwise they are currently working within your business.

We take a look at the 'who' in more detail below. The 'what' is the subject of this entire book. The 'how' part is only touched upon in this book as this topic includes detailed organizational design not relevant to this book.

Understanding the 'who'

Having the right people with the right behavioural capabilities spearheading your sales operation is a prerequisite. This applies as much to strong, professional sales management as it does to individual sales people. However, this is not just about having highly sales-trained individuals, because no amount of sales skills training or coaching will help you if you don't have people with the right combination of emotional intelligence and behavioural preference towards selling.

The key to building a strong high-performance sales team with the right capabilities and attitudes is to understand at the outset which core capabilities and personality behaviours are necessary for the role. For example, one old but still relevant question is: 'Does your business strategy and sales environment incline your approach towards having more hunters than farmers in your team, or is it the other way around?' The mix will be determined by your answers to some key questions, for example:

- Where do you plan to get new sales from? New accounts, existing accounts or acquisition?
- Are you in a high- or low-growth market segment?
- What is the cost of acquiring new customers versus retaining existing ones?
- How complex is your typical sale? Do customers require low or high levels of pre and post-sale service?
- Do you have high market share and/or high brand recognition, or are you a smaller, niche player?
- What levels of expertise and knowledge do your sales personnel require to get a foot in the door?

So, bearing these questions in mind, what should be the hunter/ farmer sales bias for your business?

New business developers – the hunters

Hunters are door-openers, motivated by pure challenge; these are the people who instinctively seek out opportunities. They are always active and focused on winning the deal. But, when the deal is in the bag, their interest fades and they are not necessarily interested in maintaining the relationship. So, hunters are often new business salespeople, but not so good at follow-through and detail.

Customer relationship nurturers – the farmers

The farmer is the cultivator of good and sustainable relationships. Generally supportive and collaborative, they are the people who engender customer loyalty by maintaining great long-term relationships. They often generate repeat business from the existing accounts that they manage.

Thinking back to the earlier description of the buying cycle for the consultative sale, it is probably fair to say that 'farmers' are most valuable in a consultative selling environment. Consultative selling usually involves significantly longer selling and buying cycles than the transactional alternative, and farmers are more comfortable with longer-term relationship building. They are more patient, and more detail-focused. However, the relatively raw energy and hunger of the hunter can play an important role, so the ideal is perhaps an amalgam of the two. That's quite hard to find and create.

Transform the sales team into value merchants

Giving away value takes no particular skill. However it's the responsibility of marketing and especially sales to get a fair return on the value delivered to customers. For most B2B companies the sales team is a substantial cost. You can't afford to let your sales team become the customer's advocate for price cuts rather than your advocate for the value your firm provides.

To determine whether your sales people are value merchants or value spendthrifts,[4] see Figure 13.3 and try answering this series of paired statements that contrast the two types. By picking the statement in each pair that best describes your salespeople, you can construct a profile of them that indicates the extent to which they are value merchants or value spendthrifts.[5]

Value compensation

As always, you get what you measure… and reward. It's important to have compensation schemes that reward value-selling behaviours and

Our salespeople:		
	a	b
1.	Routinely trade more business for lower prices	Routinely gain more business at the same price
2.	Make unsupported claims about superior value to customers	Demonstrate and document claims about superior value in monetary terms to customers
3.	Focus on the revenue/volume component of their compensation plan	Focus on the gross margin/profitability component of their compensation plan
4.	Give price concessions without changes in the market offering	Give price concessions only in exchange for cost-saving reductions in the market offering
5.	Complain that our prices are too high	Complain that our proof of superior value is lacking
6.	Give services away for free to close a deal	Strategically employ services to generate additional business
7.	Prefer to give quick price concessions to close deals and go on to other business	Are willing to hang tough in the negotiations to gain better profitability out of each deal
8.	Believe management pursues a capacity-driven strategy	Believe management pursues a value-driven strategy
9.	Sell primarily on price comparisons with competitors	Sell primarily on customer cost-of-ownership comparisons with competitors
10.	Tell us customers are only interested in price	Tell us customers insights to improve the value of our offerings

Statements reproduced with kind permission from *Value Merchants*, Anderson, J., Kumar, N. and Narus, J.; Harvard Business School Publishing; 1 Oct 2007

Figure 13.3 Are your salespeople value merchants or value spendthrifts?

profitability. We are strong advocates of defining your compensation plans based on profitability of accounts, since profitability demonstrates both delivering value to the customer and getting a decent reward for the value that has been delivered.

Profitability should be rewarded more significantly than revenue in your compensation plan. Let's give an example of why this should be. One of our customers, operating in the IT software industry, told us that when he changed to rewarding profitability, rather than revenue or volume, his salespeople suddenly stopped discounting and instead started putting together evidence of how the price was worth the slightly higher variance from their major competitor.

Naturally, you need to ensure that you're changing behaviours at the same time as changing your compensation plans. Targeting profitability isn't enough on its own, especially if you're operating in highly competitive or commoditized markets. Particularly in transactional selling, you will need to adopt TCO (total cost of ownership) tools or other value calculators. We would suggest targeting your sales people on percentage of profitability and demonstrated use of TCO models (or similar) with customers.

Your sales people will need to be trained, coached, and rewarded for value selling to ensure the desired behaviours are embedding in your organization. Training should be focused on:

- exploring what customers need, want and say they value;
- demonstrating how your organization delivers value;
- negotiating terms and conditions;
- focusing on results.

Selecting and developing sales people and teams

We know that people are predisposed to be good or not at selling. You know if you enjoy it or hate it, are good at it or terrible. Are people predisposed to be good at either consultative or transactional selling? We believe so and have worked with the developers of a world-leading behavioural tool to develop the Consultative Transactional Quotient or CTQ. The CTQ is unlike traditional psychometric instruments as it approaches human behaviour from the perspective of neuroscience, rather than psychology. It takes advantage of some of the most up-to-date neural discoveries to provide users with a series of 'maps' that enable individuals to identify the ways in which they prefer to respond to the world around them to achieve their goals. This insight also helps them to understand more about their true potential, as well as what may be hindering them from achieving even higher performance.

For more on the CTQ go to http://www.futurecurve.com/CTQ

People produce superior profits

Building on selecting, compensating and managing the right sales people is David Maister's causal model.[6] He says that to obtain superior

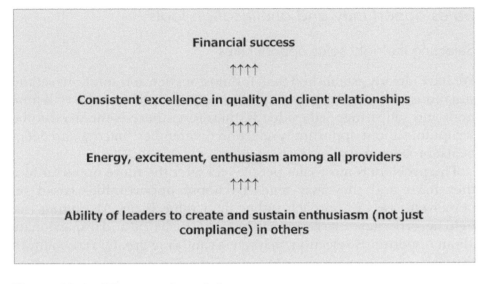

Figure 13.4 The causal model

Source: Courtesy of David Maister.

returns, don't watch the money but watch and manage the things that produce the money. His causal model is shown in Figure 13.4.

Maister demonstrated statistically in the causal model a clear path to profits and while others had discussed these links before,[7] he provided formal evidence and unveiled the critical elements of personal managerial influence, rather than formal management systems such as strategies, policies, reward systems and the like.

He concludes that the only competitive advantage, for organizations and for careers, is the ability to create and transfer drive, determination, energy, excitement and enthusiasm.

Another constant theme in Maister's work is that everything ultimately comes down to understanding how people work. His philosophy is that everything we want in life – whether it be profits, respect, fame, loyal subordinates, cooperative colleagues or, in our personal lives, love and relationships – all these things, each and every one of them, has to be given to us by another human being. That means we must know how to earn and deserve what we want the other person to give us back, and that means becoming good at relationships in everything we do. Critical therefore for consultative selling.

Sales opportunity and qualification tools

Selecting the right sales opportunities

We have already established that, for most service and solutions selling situations, the cost of pursuing sales opportunities is at an all-time high and still rising. Self-evidently, therefore, there is the need to be scrupulous about opportunity selection (remember, 'narrow and deep' beats 'broad and shallow').

The problem is most sales people feel safer the more opportunities they have, and they may tend to choose opportunities based on perceived ease of approach rather than value focus. Marketing can help here. Because marketing can be more analytical and dispassionate about opportunity selection, marketers can bring greater rationality to the task.

Considering the required process from top-level value proposition down, here is a ten-point plan:

1. Identify target sales opportunities, checking each possibility against your completed value proposition template and top-level value proposition statement.
2. Does an opportunity 'fit' the criteria of the top-level value proposition?
3. If 'No', reject it.
4. If 'Yes', scan the opportunity thoroughly. What is the opportunity size and value? Is your proposed offering strategic to the prospective customer? Do all of the numbers work? Are you able to refine the value proposition for the specific opportunity and still keep integrity and congruence with the top-level value proposition?
5. If 'No', reject it.
6. If 'Yes', change the status from opportunity to confirmed sales lead.
7. Identify those people within the confirmed sales lead organization who need to be engaged in the buying process, and create refined value proposition statements for each of them (the benefits and cost of an offering for a chief finance officer (CFO), for example, will be different from those for a chief information officer (CIO), chief marketing officer (CMO) or whoever). Do these further refinements maintain integrity and congruence with the top-level value proposition?

8. If, 'No, reject it.
9. If 'Yes', identify and create tools required to start the sales process.
10. Sell!

Who does what in this process? Well, the key to success (and sanity), we believe, is for both marketing and sales to be involved at every step of this process, but for there to be a progressive handover along the way. Thus, at the start, the involvement is marketing 90 per cent versus sales 10 per cent. At the end, the balance has shifted to marketing 10 per cent versus sales 90 per cent (see Figure 13.1).

Qualify or die

There is an elementary logic to where to target your sales efforts first – go where the money is. In financial services organizations, for example, the sales people will often focus their sales efforts on high net worth individuals.

However, irrespective of whether your customers are at the top or bottom end of the markets and no matter what your offerings are, you still have to decide who your targets and prospects are. Here are some qualifying techniques that will decrease the chances of price objections.

Research

There are numerous online sites that you can use to find company information. Hoovers.com, Dun & Bradstreet (D&B) and Experian are typical of sites that will give you information about the company and its creditworthiness. Newspapers, blogs, company websites ... the information about companies these days is extensive and readily available. Sometimes simply putting your prospect's name into a search engine can reveal information about the company and some of its key individuals.

Universities, business schools, associations and membership clubs often offer free information sources to their alumni or members. Use them!

Good question

Sometimes prospects may offer up price objections as a smokescreen for their real issue. That real issue may be something the prospect finds hard to say so they throw up price as the decoy reason. Here are a few suggestions for helping to qualify the prospect:

- Issue or need. Does the prospect have a major issue or a stated need that your offering will fulfill?
- Budget. Is this a planned purchase that has already been budgeted for, or will you have to help create a compelling business case?
- Decision making. Who is involved in the buying decision? What is the process? Can you get in front of the ultimate decision maker (to avoid your prospect having to defer to a higher authority)?

Follow the process

Sales people don't get paid for attending sales meetings, they get paid for making a sale. If the qualification questions above don't get asked, then frankly your sales people are wasting their time and yours. Before even setting a meeting, your people really should ensure that your prospect has an identified issue or need, has the budget and has the appropriate authority to buy. No one likes wasted effort and time.

Offering management

The last part of this section picks up where we left off in Chapter 7. We said there are four steps to managing your offerings, which are:

1. Understand and categorize the offerings that you currently have (Chapter 7).
2. Put in place an offering management process (OMP), including the people to manage it. This should include an innovation and new offering development process.
3. Using your OMP, identify where your offerings are in the offering lifecycle (see Figure 7.1), including those that should be retired.
4. Develop new offerings.

In this chapter we go through Steps 2, 3 and 4 which are about offering management.

Step 2. Offering management process

Once the mapping and categorizing of existing offerings is complete (as shown in Chapter 7), you can move on to address how you will develop, introduce and institutionalize an offering management process (Figure 13.5). Although we are not describing in detail an offering lifecycle process in this book, here are some key points to focus on.

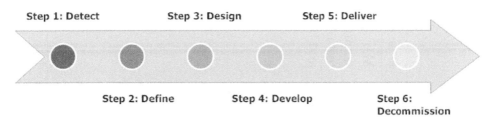

Figure 13.5   Offering management process

The full process, for creating an offering from scratch, involves six steps: detect, define, design, develop, deliver and decommission (Table 13.1). It may be, of course, that you need to 'retro-fit' an existing offering, in which case it may be appropriate to start at Step 2 because the Step 1 'go/no go' decision has self-evidently already been made.

Organizing and managing offering developments

Establish a standard offering assessment and development process so that your organization can compare different opportunities fairly, on an equal basis.

To proceed or not to proceed?

Offering assessment and development needs to be as much about eliminating ideas as adopting them. Research shows that the cost of pursuing sales opportunities is at an all-time high and rising. Because an offering is at the heart of a sales opportunity, it is important to be sure that a proposed offering is what the market, or segment, or

Table 13.1 Offering management process in more detail

Detect	Define	Design	Develop	Deliver	Decommission
Seek out an opportunity and create the high-level case. If it stands up to review against defined criteria, proceed to…	Further test the idea by investing the time needed to put some flesh on the bones of the offering. If it stands up to review against defined criteria, proceed to…	This is the stage where much more detail is required. Flesh the idea fully and, if it still stands up, proceed to…	When an offering gets to this stage, a full development plan is required. Stages 1, 2 and 3 have focused on the offering itself. Here, we also look at the delivery requirements in order to develop a full launch plan. Is the offering still viable? If it is, it's time to go to …	Market commitment: test marketing and beyond.	It is important to recognize when an offering has reached the end of its useful life (otherwise it will drain energy and resources), and decommission/retire it.

prospect wants or needs, that it is congruent with your identified value experience, and that the entire value proposition is viable.

So, at the end of each step of the offering development process and before moving to the next step, there is the need to make a 'go/no go' decision. These are the milestones. Be ruthless about your choices because, to go to market, you need to be sure that an offering really will fly.

The gateways to development

Making good 'go/no go' decisions requires you to define the 'gateways' at the end of each step. Here are some examples of 'gateway questions':

- Is there a valid business case for this development offering?
- Will the offering provide adequate return with acceptable risks?
- Is the offering or programme aligned with our company strategy?
- Is continued investment in the offering development or research and development (R&D) project warranted?
- Are we addressing all of the significant issues?
- Are the project plan and request for resources sound?
- Does this project have a high priority relative to other offering portfolio opportunities?

To help keep the whole process focused and objective it is valuable to create an offering Assessment Committee of some kind. You need sufficient gate reviews to ensure that an offering is viable, but not so many that it adds unnecessarily to the overhead of the development process and slows things down. Each review requires the team to create or update the project information and develop a presentation, which may involve quite a lot of work. For greatest efficiency, therefore, place gateway reviews at points in the process prior to where there are major commitments of resources or funds or major risks, eg design, building, advertising and launch costs, and so on.

The information needed for successful gateway reviews includes: market definition, opportunity and forecast; key customer needs; offering/product definition; offering/product strategy; technology and intellectual property plan/issues; delivery methodologies or manufacturing and supply chain plan/issues; marketing plan/issues;

project budget and schedule; business case, projected profit and return on investment; project risks; regulatory, environmental and safety issues.

Who makes the decisions?

A senior team needs to make the 'go/no go' decisions at the gates. Choose a cross-section from different functional areas, but they must be able to commit resources. To prevent unfair selection, the team needs to be made to operate according to a pre-set list of criteria and rules – they can't play favourites! The roles of this senior management team include:

- developing product strategy;
- managing product portfolio;
- managing overall product development resources;
- conducting phase/stage-gate reviews;
- monitoring overall performance;
- addressing critical issues with development programmes.

What are the typical gate criteria?

Typically, the team needs to make judgements across a whole range of decision criteria, including:

- Strategic alignment. Does the proposed offering fit with the company's strategic alignment? Does it leverage competencies and capabilities? And does it support balance, overall?
- Product advantage. What customer needs does the offering meet? What are the unique benefits?
- Market attractiveness. What is the size of the market/segment, and what is the growth potential?
- Technical feasibility. Are the technical aspects of the offering practical and feasible? Are there any technical gaps, or complexity, or technical risk?
- Risk. What are the risks? In particular, is it possible to manage the risks? Are you sure there are no show-stoppers?

- Return. How profitable will this offering be? What is the estimated return versus risk? And can the sales forecasts and cost targets be met?
- Regulatory. Does the proposed offering satisfy all necessary legal requirements and policies?

The Big 1-2-3 Key to this process is:

1. Having the right group of people on the decision or review panel.
2. Clear decision factors that are linked back to the business strategy.
3. Having the appropriate resources (people, time, money, materials etc) available to proceed to the next stage or gate.

Step 3. Offering life cycle mapping

Map your offering on the offering life cycle (Figure 13.6).

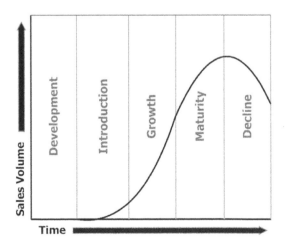

Figure 13.6 Offering life cycle

The offering life cycle asserts four things:

- Offerings have a limited life.
- Offering sales pass through distinct stages, each posing a different challenge to the seller.
- Profits rise and fall at different stages in the offering life cycle.
- Offerings require different marketing, financial, manufacturing or service development/delivery, purchasing and people strategies in each stage of their life cycle.

This is a major task and since this is a topic that warrants a book in itself, we commend the full and excellent explanation of identifying where your offering are and mapping them, given in *Marketing Management: Analysis, Implementation and Control* by Philip Kotler (Prentice Hall, 9th edition, 1999) and numerous other excellent product strategy and management books.

It is important to be quite ruthless about decommissioning decisions. Decide what offerings need to go. Look at what's selling and what isn't, what is profitable and what isn't. Decide what to do with old offerings. Bear in mind that there may be innovative ways to capitalize on them by, for example, expanding into new territories, selling them on, or selling the licenses to others to exploit in new, different areas. Here's an example of just such an initiative – how HP manages new uses for old technology by not completely retiring old patents, but by selling them on.

HP finds creative applications for patched up patents[8]

By John Murray Brown, FT, 29 August 2008

When John O'Dea went to see Hewlett-Packard to discuss whether there might be any patents he could license, he came away with an agreement to use the core technologies behind one of the US company's best known products – its thermal inkjet printer.

At first sight, the collaboration between HP and Crospon, a small medical devices company in the west of Ireland, is not unusual. All big technology companies are combing their patent portfolios to see whether they can license inventions and recover some of the vast investments they make in research and development.

What was eye-catching in this case though was that an idea developed for one industry is being exploited in another quite unrelated one. HP's printer technology will be applied as part of a transdermal skin patch for drug delivery, which its promoters claim might one day replace the hypodermic syringe.

The story shows that large technology companies are far from precious about their inventions. HP has a portfolio of nearly 30,000 patents, some registered long ago but never generating a commercial return. At HP Labs, the company's central research facility, it has an active programme to identify new uses for these old technologies. HP does not disclose how much it makes in annual royalties and fees from such arrangements, but it is believed to be about $500m.

In the jargon this is referred to as 'repurposing'. Charlie Chapman, director in the intellectual property (IP) licensing office in its Palo Alto headquarters, says HP scientists have also looked at using the printer technology for a fuel injection system for cars.

The idea of a skin patch, he says, was first developed by HP Labs several years ago but was dropped because of the perceived regulatory hurdles of bringing such a product to market. Instead, it decided to look for outside partners.

It was Enterprise Ireland, an Irish government agency charged with fostering innovation and technology links between multi-nationals and indigenous Irish companies, that brought the two together.

'HP had a programme to license out their IP. But they wouldn't have thought of Ireland if we hadn't approached them', says Michael Moriarty, head of innovation and global partnering at EI, which has an office in Palo Alto.

'When we visited, HP had come up with a list of seven or eight of these things, and this one was floating out there as a ninth thing. But they weren't really talking about it because they were thinking they might do a spin-out themselves', Mr O'Dea recalls of the first meeting.

Crospon is now developing the product for general drug use, but at the time it was working on an insulin delivery system for use in hospitals for diabetes sufferers. 'I was looking for an intravenous technology, but I came away with a transdermal one', says Mr O'Dea.

One of the first things that struck him about the printer technology was that it offered the possibility of administering more than one drug. This was critical for diabetes patients, as the weakness of traditional delivery systems such as pumps is they often overdose or under-dose a patient. With a patch that could deliver more than one drug, a patient could receive both insulin and glycogen, which counteracts insulin's effects.

Until now, transdermal patches such as those used for nicotine programmes or hormone supplements have relied on the substance being absorbed through the skin, rather than introduced directly into the bloodstream. The HP patch, which is controlled by a microprocessor, uses micro needles, which just penetrate the skin's surface. The tiny syringes feel more like the lick of a cat than a traditional hypodermic.

The prototype Mr O'Dea shows visitors is a one-inch square device containing nine tiny reservoirs, each capable of holding a different drug. A special polymer material is heated up when a dose is scheduled for delivery. This causes the polymer to expand. Like the plunger in a syringe it pushes against a membrane holding the drug. This ruptures, creating the momentum to release the liquid into the skin.

He says there are about four other companies like Crospon engaged in development, some using electric current to open pores in the skin, others deploying ultrasonics. But he believes the HP technology has several key advantages. Just as the inkjet printer can use different colours, HP's smart patch can administer a cocktail of drugs to order – in individual dosages, predetermined by a doctor, at prescribed times.

Mr O'Dea is in discussions with pharmaceuticals companies about what the optimum size for the prototype is. He envisages it will be possible to put as many as 400 separate reservoirs on a single patch. 'But that's the sort of knowledge the pharma companies have.'

The agreement with HP involves three separate patents and the transfer of various technical knowhow. HP will earn a royalty on production. It will also benefit if Crospon were eventually to sell on the business or be taken over.

'It's a risk sharing. We both benefit if it meets its objectives. If it doesn't, we'll both have put in costs', says Mr O'Dea.

He thinks there are about three or four years of laboratory work still to do before the patch becomes commercially available, adding: 'The link-up has done nothing but good in terms of our profile. You only have to Google us. But at the end of the day you are only as good as the products you deliver.'

© The Financial Times Limited 2008

Step 4. New offerings

Only when your existing offerings have been defined and catalogued should you think about creating new offerings.

New offering creation brings its own challenges. Key is an innovation process, to capture and evaluate new ideas from around the company, your customers and your suppliers. Many of the innovations thrown up by such processes are less about completely new offerings but often about enhancing existing ones, making them work better, faster, more productively, even cheaper. Remember too that new offerings are frequently found by changing the constituent parts of 'the whole product' discussed earlier and shown in Figure 13.7.

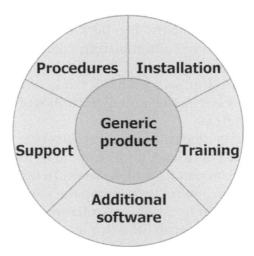

Figure 13.7　A whole product map for a technology product

Source: modified from *Crossing the Chasm*, Geoffrey A. Moore, HarperCollins, 1991

So you must put in place and proactively manage an innovation and ideas process. If you sit back and wait for ideas to come to your attention, and then discard the one or two you might get, you'll feel disillusioned and your organization will not flourish. But, if you put in place a proactive process, within a couple of years you'll find that it becomes institutionalized and will provide you with real value.

Once a possible new offering has been identified, take it through the process already described for sifting existing offerings.

New strategic tools

We are sure there will emerge many innovate and creative ways of applying value propositions for strategic decision making. This is an ongoing discussion[9] where we hope online collaboration will yield useful new models. Here are just two such ideas.

A portfolio of value propositions

On a high floor in the Barclays Bank building in London's Canary Wharf, a conversation took place with Jonathan Rose, the bank's commercial director for global retail and commercial banking. It was around the time that the true extent of the 2008 financial crisis was becoming apparent. Lehmann Brothers had gone. Leading banks all around the world were contemplating taking government help to stay afloat. And we were discussing how banks might best serve their customers. Jonathan Rose said: 'What if banks could change so as to manage their businesses on the basis of portfolios of value propositions – wouldn't that be great!'

Well, yes, it would be, and it helped launch a very animated discussion. Here's the gist of it. Think back for a moment to the Boston Matrix. It is a long-established marketing tool. A classic. Developed by the Boston Consulting Group, the matrix helps companies audit and classify their products and services in terms of performance, and acts as a guide to investment. The two measures (the two axes of the box) are market share and market growth (Figure 13.8).

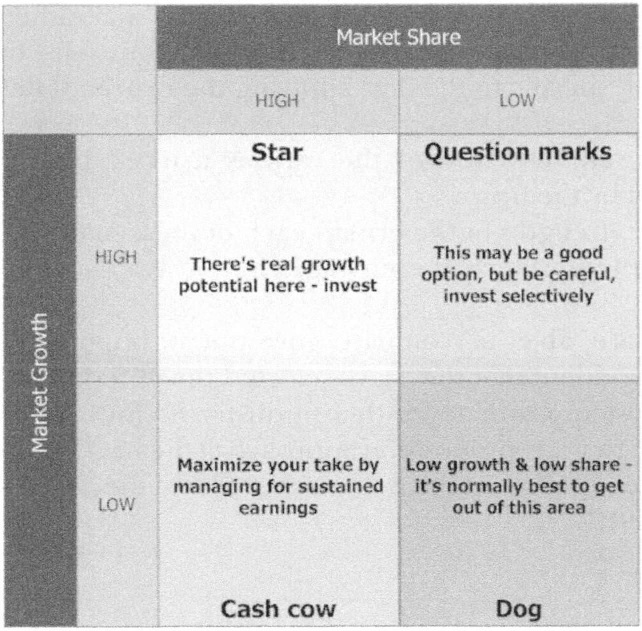

Figure 13.8 The Boston matrix

The Boston Box approach is sometimes criticized for relying on two single factors: relative market share and market growth. To overcome this difficulty, General Electric, McKinsey and others jointly developed a multifactor approach using the same fundamental ideas as the Boston Consulting Group. They used market attractiveness and business strengths as the two main axes and built up these dimensions from a number of weighted variables.

Using these variables, and a scheme for weighting them according to their importance, markets (or businesses) are classified into one of nine cells in a three-by-three matrix. Thus, the same purpose is served as in the Boston Matrix (ie comparing investment opportunities among markets or businesses) but with the difference that multiple criteria are used. These criteria vary according to circumstances.

The GE Matrix has since been developed by Professor Malcolm McDonald to form a simple but effective version consisting of four boxes. The four-box Directional Policy Matrix (DPM) defines business strengths in terms of critical success factors (CSFs).

The key difference from the Boston Matrix is that rather than using only two variables, the criteria which are used for each axis are totally relevant and specific to the firm applying the matrix. It demonstrates:

- Relative attractiveness of the various markets based on criteria selected by the firm.
- Relative strengths of the firm in each of these markets.
- Relative importance of each market.

Managers are able to compare investment opportunities among markets, confident that they have selected the criteria for comparison that are most appropriate for their industry. So for organizations that are adopting a value proposition approach at the heart of their business model, one of these critical axes should be the value experience (Figure 13.9).

		Value Experience	
		HIGH	LOW
Market or Functional Growth	HIGH	**High value, high differentiation** In a worthwhile market sector where you are able to demonstrate high value-experience, your VP will resonate very highly	**High value potential** If the market sector is of high potential it will be worth your investing to build your value-experience to strengthen the VP
	LOW	With strong value-experience it will be relatively straighforward to keep and satisfy customers **Good return for relatively low investment**	Don't even bother - there's no VP here **A waste of time**

Figure 13.9 A value experience matrix

As Jonathan Rose said:

> If the top-level value proposition is at the heart of your business model, and if it is appropriately and congruently expressed right through the organization and out to the customers, it then becomes possible to ensure that the business delivers targeted customer experiences, profitably. Banks have, for a long time, been criticized for their product-silo thinking, whereby customers run the risk of being just a bunch of account numbers. The value proposition approach offers a way out of this.

As banks emerge from the current financial crisis, perhaps they'll realize that the time has actually come to operate differently with their customers.

Crossing the technology chasm

In Chapter 7 we talked of the notion of the whole product and how this is very important in both product and services organizations. Geoffrey Moore's assertion in *Crossing the Chasm* is that you need to convince the early majority to purchase (the folks after the early adopters in the 'diffusion of innovation' curve[10]). To do this you need to build the whole product – a complete solution to a real-life problem, with all the necessary pieces in place to deliver all the value of the solution. And for technology companies, this is not about delivering the technology but rather about delivering the whole value experience.

When John Woodget talks about the research Intel has done into Gen Y consumers and their expectations of a seamless experience across all their internet devices, we liken this to a good example of how Intel have 'crossed the chasm'.[11] Intel needs to convince both the early and late majority to buy their products (see Chapter 11).

How have they done this? By focusing on the full user value experience and ultimately the value proposition, not just the technology. What Intel is offering is not merely the power or speed of its chips but what can be experienced through having its chips in a variety of devices. Gen Y wants seamless collaboration so that's what Gen Y will get.

But for most of the technology-centric developers, the concept of actually doing what a large community of people really want runs counter to their whole way of thinking, especially when they focus their efforts mostly on the early adopter avant-garde. The result: they miss the early majority, not because the early adopters are too distracted or busy, but because they never built something that the early majority wanted anyway. Adoption of the value proposition approach is a surefire way to get them across the chasm.

Notes

1. http://davidmaister.com/blog/176/Values-in-Action—new-free-seminar.
2. *It's not easy going green*, Knowledge@Wharton, February 2007.
3. 'Ending the War Between Sales and Marketing', Philip Kotler, Neil Rackham and Suj Krishnaswamy, *Harvard Business Review*, July 2006.
4. Reprinted by permission of Harvard Business School Press. From *Value Merchants*, J. Anderson, N. Kumar and J. Narus, Boston, MA, 2007. Copyright © 2007 by the Harvard Business School Publishing Corporation; all rights reserved.
5. For an online version of the Value Merchants or Value Spendthrifts diagnostic tool, go to www.futurecurve.com.
6. *David Maister, Practice What You Preach*, Free Press, 2001.
7. *The Service Profit Chain* by James L. Heskett, W. Earl Sasser and Leonard A. Schlesinger.
8. Quoted with permission of *The Financial Times*, 2008.
9. Join the discussion at www.valueproposition.biz.
10. *Diffusion of Innovations*, Everett Rogers, Simon & Schuster International; 5th revised edition 2003.
11. *Crossing The Chasm*, Geoffrey A. Moore; HarperCollins, 1991.

14 Starting and sustaining

Congratulations! You've got this far. So the big question that one normally asks at this stage is, 'OK, so what do I do on Monday morning?' Here's our starter on what to do next and how you can sustain your value propositions.

Are the conditions right?

Before moving on to look at the process steps, let's take a few minutes to examine if you have the right conditions to start.

Examine strengths not weaknesses

Take a lesson from Sir Clive Woodward, the England national rugby union team manager who managed the England side to victory at the 2003 Rugby World Cup. Focus on first thinking that your company or business unit can be very successful and harbour a team of winners, and you will be. The correct positive thinking will turn into belief which will turn into positive outcomes. Sounds simple? Yes, but how many companies truly focus on their strengths and celebrate them? So rather than picking at the weaknesses, which has dire consequences for morale, instead shout about the successes and create a culture that breeds positive, winning thinking.

Change your measurement and reward system

Look at how you want to reward value by rewarding profitability. Remember what gets measured gets done, but focus on measuring the outputs or more importantly the outcomes of your value proposition (VP). For example, measure the increase in profitability or the number of customers retained. Ideally measure and monitor through a balanced scorecard.

Change the reward system of all customer-facing staff, especially sales people, to focus them on selling profitably and not purely on revenue. Also share targets among all customer-facing staff to encourage team thinking and behaviour.

Exercise customer selectivity

Focus on matching the customers that you want to your value proposition and not serving everyone who wants to be your customer.

Shelter from the storm

If these ideas are new and you are putting them together and actioning them for the first time, focus on one discrete business area or product line or market sector. Ideally one unit that you can easily identify that is away from others. When any change happens, and this will be a big change, people react against change. For the VP process to be successful and develop a footprint across the entire business (and not just stay as an interesting project we tried once), then you need an incubator – a part of the business in which to make this work and be a success.

Provide leadership

A strong sponsor is critical. One organization of our acquaintance started off their value proposition work with great enthusiasm and focused energy. Then the project sponsor became distracted and turned his attention to other things. The consequence? The value champions in the team got bogged down in the detail and missed the big picture. Focus drifted back to old habits and paths of least resistance, resulting in weak value challenges, platitudes and all the other areas of non-differentiation. Your leader and sponsor must be senior in your organization and must be genuinely engaged and in it for the long-haul.

The weather system

Fred Wiersema[1] talks of the common ground or the weather systems that dominate a company and create conducive environmental conditions. He identified two conditions necessary for endemic change: a sense of urgency and an uplifting team spirit. Trying to change without these he says is like 'trying to breathe in a vacuum' and their importance cannot be underestimated. 'Urgency,' he says, 'is not about rushing. A sense of urgency induces people to learn faster, correct mistakes more aggressively, and strive to find innovative applications. If something is worth striving for, it's worth striving for with fervor and zeal.' Hear, hear we say! We have worked as advisors with many organizations where we have known sometimes before the project had even started that the organization didn't have the appetite, wasn't hungry enough, eager or keen enough for this work to be a success. Teamwork is very important here, as is energy – the energy of the organization and the energy of the teams to create something bigger and better than they started with.

Starting the process

1. Get your Board on board – this is vital to achieve consensus and clarity about strategy and direction [link back to strategic alignment]. Conduct interviews of Board members and consensus workshops.
2. Get focus into your strategic programmes. It is likely that you will already have various initiatives on the go that, when looked at together, can be used as the basis to start building your value proposition. You need to map all of your strategic programmes clearly and go beyond mere project or programme design to consider the totality of your business, or area of focus. Use this mapping process as a master change programme and it will also help you

with initiative rationalization and can highlight duplication, gaps and irrelevancies.

3. Pull a project team together, drawn from your best people right across the organization
4. Appoint a strong project manager reporting to the chief executive officer (CEO) (ensuring CEO is genuine key sponsor).
5. Work with an experienced external organization to guide you through the process, especially when it comes to understanding your customer value experience.
6. Ensure pace and buy-in right from the start.

Building your value proposition

Market

You need to ask yourself the following key questions before moving into traditional market segmentation:

- What are my primary ways of delivering value to my customers?
- Where, therefore, are the most promising market spaces for my organization?
- What are the most important capabilities my organization has or must have to create and deliver value?

Then:

- Define your markets.
- Map your markets.
- Understand who the decision makers in your markets are and what they purchase.
- Understand why decision makers purchase (and how to meet their needs).
- Form market segments that work for you by combining like-minded decision makers.

Value experience

You need to ascertain and understand:

- What do your customers value?
- Of these, which areas have priority over others, and why?
- Which competitors or alternatives measure up to these areas of value?
- How does your organization stack up?
- What are the costs and benefits experienced by your customers in the process?

To elicit this information, we suggest the following areas of questioning:

- Background to relationship.
- Value.
- Cost (including price and risk).
- Offerings.
- Marketplace.
- Competition and alternatives.
- Recommendations and suggestions.

Offerings

You need to be able to understand how your offerings deliver value to your customers. You need to:

- Understand and categorize what you have in your current portfolio.
- Put in place an offer life cycle process (OLP) and system of management including the people to manage it. This should include an innovation and new offer development process.
- Evaluate through the OLP the offerings to be retired.
- Develop new offerings.
- Understand the cost to you and your organization of creating the new offerings.

Benefits

To understand how the value experience delivers key benefits to your customers, you will need to go through the benefits mapping exercise shown in Chapter 8. Separate out those benefits that customers expect to receive from those they didn't expect but found of significant additional benefit.

Alternatives and differentiation

Once you understand what customers truly value, have prioritized them, understood how your offerings deliver that value, and at what cost; then you can start to understand the competing alternatives available to your customers. If the alternatives include direct competitors to your organization, you should define how you are different from, and better than, those competitors by addressing the following points:

- Which alternatives can deliver the best value to my customers?
- In what time frame?
- Are my competitors able to deliver value this cheaper, faster, better than my organization?
- What makes my organization different from and better than my competition?
- What does the overall competitive landscape look like?
- How do my offerings give me competitive advantage with my customers? How can I combine them to best effect to marginalize my competitors?

Proof

Customers require evidence of your capability and value, hence the need to track and measure your value:

- Create case studies.
- Write a book.
- Develop articles for use on- and offline.
- Publish customer testimonials.
- Measure and track the impact of your value proposition. Implement a benefits realization programme to measure the effectiveness of your VP over time.
- The output of this measurement can be used and built into a value calculator. Technology companies often use total cost of ownership (TCO) tools or spreadsheets to demonstrate to clients the true

total cost of purchase over the purchase lifetime. This is often used as part of a return on investment calculation that may go into a building a business case for the purchase of the item or service.

- For more information on TCO tools for use in product companies, see www.tcotoolbox.com

Create your value proposition template and write your value proposition statement

Now take the outputs of the six process steps and begin to populate your template. Table 14.1 is a recap of the template from Chapter 11.

Remember that one of the outputs from the value proposition process or VPP is the value proposition statement. This is not the boilerplate or elevator pitch for your firm, and not to be used externally. It is the foundation upon which your value rests. As we quoted in Chapter 2, Lanning[2] says:

A value proposition is:

- *about* customers but for your organization;
- not addressed to customers but must drive these communications;
- articulates the essence of a business, defining exactly what the organization fully intends to make happen in the customer's life.

Ways to use your value proposition

Message development

Your value proposition will help to ensure consistency of messages right across your organization and out into your customers. You must:

- Prioritize your messages via the benefits map.
- Sub-refine via the difference–value matrix.
- Create a framework and hierarchy, based on emotional/political/ rational analysis.
- Develop a message ladder – where buyers, offerings, and messages meet.
- Add in the communications channel.

Table 14.1 Ten-point value proposition template

Ten-point value proposition template	Corresponding areas in Figure 2.4	Functional responsibility
1 Who is the intended customer?	Market	VP team with Board sponsor
2 What will the customer's experience be of the offering and the company, and what price will they pay?	Value experience	VP team with Board sponsor
3 What offerings will we create to deliver the intended experience to the intended customer? What purchase or usage of offerings do we want from the intended customer?	Offerings	VP team with Board sponsor
4 What benefits will the customer derive from the experience and at what cost?	Benefits	VP team with Board sponsor
5 What competing alternatives do the customers have? How are we different?	Alternatives & differentiation	VP team with Board sponsor
6 How will we substantiate our ability to deliver the resulting customer experience measurably and specifically?	Proof	VP team with Board sponsor
7 Over what time frame will the proposition be delivered to the customer?		VP team with Board sponsor
8 How will the value proposition be communicated internally and externally?		Marketing & sales
9 How will the value proposition be operationalized throughout the business?		Operations & HR
10 How will we measure and monitor the effectiveness of the proposition on our business?		Balanced scorecard and finance

Sales and marketing tools

Use your value proposition to help qualify sales opportunities and to offer buyers value at every stage of the buying cycle.

Alignment of value across your organization is critical for long-term profitability and benefits. This is not a quick fix and requires leadership and organizational design skills. Alignment needs to be with customers, with your people, with suppliers, and with channel partners.

Sustaining the lead

It is not the strongest of the species that survives, nor the most intelligent, but rather the one most responsive to change.

(Charles Darwin)

To stay ahead you have to monitor and refresh to get better and better. Building a value proposition isn't a one-off activity. Now that you've done the hard work, don't let it all fade and die but keep it alive through regular updating and review. Every three months throughout every year monitor and review one or more aspects of your value proposition. As your value proposition is modified, you also must ensure that any corresponding operations are also modified.

For example, if your customer value experience research tells you that customers are unhappy having to wait a week for delivery of an item they have ordered, you ensure that customer service telephone staff inform customers how long an item will take to deliver at the time of ordering. Because an item was in stock, customers were assuming that it would be dispatched immediately, whereas in reality, the whole dispatch and postal service was taking a week. Through your research, you determine that customers are very happy as long as they know this in advance. This must be operationalized through the sales, customer service, warehousing and dispatch teams. A simple review plan is shown in Figure 14.1.

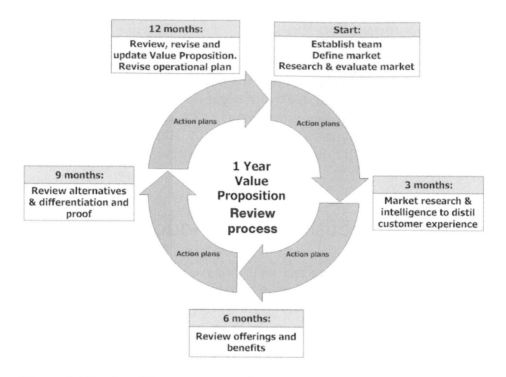

Figure 14.1   A rolling one-year value proposition review process

And finally...

Remember our film producer at the beginning of this book? By recognizing that the value experience of his clients centred on giving them clarity and understanding around their strategic intent and goals, and enabling them to communicate these aspects with feeling, the corporate film producer who we introduced at the start of this book changed his approach fundamentally.

He still makes films, but they are created through workshops in which executives are guided to review and explain their motivations and aspirations from a gut level. The outputs have genuine power because they are demonstrably 'real'. They are particularly valuable in and for multinational organizations where English is not the first language of many of the staff, because emotional clarity communicates itself whatever the language.

This enables our film producer to present his organization as a 'message facilitator'. The 'market' for his work is with large, often global, organizations who need to achieve alignment of vision, strategy and value proposition around the world, around the clock.

In addition to a film, the outputs always include a 'message file' that can be used by the client as a briefing document for other communications agencies. This, self-evidently, multiplies the value of the work.

Notes

1. *Customer Intimacy*, Fred Wiersema, Knowledge Exchange, 1996.
2. *Delivering Profitable Value*, Michael J. Lanning, Perseus Publishing, 1998.

15 The value-focused enterprise

Organizations are paid to create value, not control costs.

(Peter Drucker)

We've introduced the idea of the value proposition, at the top level, as a focal component of the business model: which is to say, it is the central role of a business to create and deliver its value proposition. It is the only way a business can prosper. Failure to create and deliver value means the business itself fails. And, because Value = Benefits minus Cost (where cost includes financial price and any risk factors), value creation and delivery crucially depends on benefits realization and cost transparency.

We are talking about an entire business ethos: the value-focused enterprise (VFE).

In fact, failure to create a VFE risks allowing 'value' to shrivel to the status of the dreaded 'benefits statement', and a series of undifferentiated 'push' marketing slogans of the 'buy our service because it's best' type. The comparison can be made again here between total quality management and the quality focused enterprise and where quality is merely inspected in at the end of a production cycle.

Operating a business as a VFE is a big deal. Frequently it requires major change, and change can be threatening and hard to implement. The requirement, as we set out to show in this chapter, is for the creation of a flexible, dynamic organization capable of responding quickly to market signals. It's a topic that has been in the air for several years under various titles – the agile enterprise, the dynamic enterprise, the collaborative enterprise, the extended enterprise, and on and on.

Most people can see the sense of this. Making it happen is a whole other story.

The theory is straightforward enough: if you want an organization to be receptive and responsive to market, economic and political signals, you have to inculcate a through-organization alignment of understanding about what it stands for (the value proposition) and discriminately devolve power to all levels to allow appropriate, responsive value creation to flourish.

The trouble is, this can scare the pants off an awful lot of people, not least those at the top. So let's just review the situation to – we hope – convince you that changing to a VFE, scary as it may be, is worth the effort.

Check the rulebook: it's different now

Let's start by going right back to basics. Where does business value come from? The answer to this question is the key to unlocking future success. And, significantly, the answer has changed in the recent past.

As we pointed out in Chapter 1, the all-powerful business model that grew out of the Industrial Revolution and reached its peak in the mid- and late 20th century recently fell over dead. But human nature being what it is, we can all too easily tend to cling to the comforting familiarity of ideas that have outlived their usefulness.

Under the old rules, business value came from power: industry position, market share, territorial dominance, control of precious resources, secret knowledge, rights of seniority, and the like. Might was right. Command and control ruled.

Then everything changed. New technology made all manner of new things and connections possible. This meant that special knowledge, in the sense that it had formerly operated, no longer provided corporate security. Whatever product or service a company chose to launch, the competition could get a 'me-too' out there in no time.

So the most prized resources became speed of innovation and response, coordination of systems, and the ability to create value on a synergistic basis with customers, suppliers and workforces.

A key outcome of this change is that decisions now need to be made and managed dynamically, always closer to the customer in any transaction. And those decisions must be made on a timely basis.

Opportunities arrive within ever narrower time frames. The options are stark. Deliver, or watch the value-creating chances pass by to be scooped up by competitors.

The required response is clear. Provide greater empowerment for people to make decisions fast. Referring decisions back for approval may forfeit corporate agility, enabling competitors to steal several marches.

But if more people in the organization are mandated to make decisions and the requirement to make them faster, how can you be sure that the decisions they make are the right ones? That is the big question.

Decision making, value creation and the CEO paradox

As just established, the key is in decision making because that is where value is created or destroyed. The consequences, for good or ill, of decision making are always dramatic, but may be particularly so where a business has to bet on long-term outcomes. So, in the great downturn of 2008/09, although the conditions did not help any car manufacturers, they caused particular problems for the US Big Three (General Motors, Ford, Daimler Chrysler). This is partly because of historical issues (for example, pension reserves) but it is partly because of a failure to identify and respond to consumer trends and preferences with sufficient accuracy or speed. And where a multiyear time to market for a new model is concerned, that is extremely bad news. Arguably, greater effort to identify upcoming customer experience preferences (and translating them into types of vehicles, and price points) would have substantially changed the outcomes.

So, decision making is the basis of resource allocation and dictates the speed at which strategies can be executed. Organizations make countless decisions on a continuous basis, from the solution of simple operational problems to the resolution of complex issues involving trade-offs between multiple and sometimes conflicting objectives. It is the cumulative effect of these decisions that creates corporate performance.

Enlightened organizations realize that better decisions do not come from greater control, but from better coordination. These enterprises accept that they cannot tell employees what to do in all circumstances. Conditions change too fast for that. Decision making needs to be based on broader guidelines. They understand that an environment which promotes the right decisions is critical to executing strategies and maximizing shareholder value. They are, in fact, VFEs.

In such organizations, the position of the business leader is somewhat paradoxical. He or she needs to be, at one and the same time, absolutely essential to the enterprise... and entirely unnecessary.

That is, leadership is no longer about command and control. It is about enablement. Having chosen good people at every level of the enterprise, the leader empowers them to use their intelligence, energy and enthusiasm, day in and day out, for the good of the organization. So an excellent leader doesn't need to be there to issue orders and check up on everything.

As a matter of fact, this has always been the case. The Duke of Wellington surveyed his 3-mile front through the rain at Waterloo, Belgium, from the strategic height at Mont St Jean. Below, he deployed Blücher, Reille, Bülow, the Duke of Orange and 67,000 others to overcome deficits of 7,000 men and 90 guns and get the day's business done by 9.15 pm. He saw no reason to function as a traffic cop. Neither should you. You have more important work to do at a strategic level.

However, this kind of hands-off leadership only works if the entire workforce understands what the organization stands for and does. In other words, when everyone understands the top-level value proposition, and is able to interpret it congruently down through all of the levels of the organization and out to clients. Which is to say, it's no use if the value proposition at 35,000 feet doesn't fit with the value proposition down at ground level where the workforce – including salespeople – are creating the value that makes it live. But when the value statements are congruent, every man and woman in the enterprise can operate as though the leader were sitting right by them all of the time.

It's a situation eloquently articulated[1] by John Chambers, chief executive officer (CEO) of Cisco, the world's largest provider of internet networking and communications equipment. As the article reports:

> Cisco is able to predict trends six to eight years ahead even in the highly volatile technology market by recognizing early-warning signals

its customers unwittingly give off. To capitalize on these 'market shifts', Chambers gave up his command-and-control style and made decision making highly collaborative. Now, an organization that used to carry out one or two cross-company initiatives a year can successfully handle dozens at a time.

John Chambers says: 'We couldn't possibly deal with one or two big priorities – let alone 22 – unless we figured out a way to work together quickly'; and later: 'The process changes are as significant and as important to the success of this collaborative model as the technology. To me, collaborative management means putting a lot of people who speak a common language to work towards a common goal.'

This devoutly-to-be-wished condition is summarized succinctly as 'alignment'.

Decisive value-creating companies kick sand in the face of ditherers

But only if they make the right decisions. Can we determine what constitutes a 'right decision' and ensure that this is the only kind of decision that people make?

The first part is easy. The going gets more complex thereafter. The right decision is one that maximizes benefits and value to both the organization and decision maker. (Identical goals in the fully aligned and thus value-focused enterprise.) And it must achieve those ends while being consistent with the organization's credo and strategy. Therefore, right decision making is always consistent with the enterprise's top-level value proposition.

The process leading to this outcome can be termed 'value-focused decision making'. It sounds like plain common sense, so it will come as no surprise that many organizations do not achieve it. Why? Because they are not aligned and therefore cannot focus their activities upon the creation of value.

Alignment is the condition where the objectives of an organization are consistent with those of its shareholders, employees and customers. It is at this point where people feel ownership of the objectives for which they are accountable. And it is this sense of ownership that provides the basis to meet the challenges of today's business environment. Think of a tug-of-war team. If they don't get behind one another and put all their weight into pulling in the same direction in a straight line, they'll all end up face down, eating mud.

The fully aligned organization has one paramount and unifying objective: maximizing customer value and thereby maximizing shareholder value. But this can't be achieved simply by implementing new tools or changing culture. It takes an appreciation of what alignment really means and the levers necessary to reach it. Organizations that understand this do three things which separate their performance from organizations that don't.

They translate strategy into a market-responsive governance model that clearly articulates decision rights: who makes which decisions and what fiscal boundaries, ethical considerations, corporate beliefs and behaviours are the parameters within which they must be made. They focus people upon the execution of the strategy by providing the direction and motivation to make the right decisions, act upon them and take ownership of results. They establish the capability for strategy actually to be executed by providing the necessary information, insight and ability to make right decisions.

Enterprises that are truly value-focused in this way employ capabilities that create a dynamic work ethic that permeates every level of the organization. Check any workforce member from the chief down to the janitor of the most remote company site and you will find a number of key commonalities of attitude:

- Business owner mentality. People are encouraged and expected to act as if they own the show. The decisions they make concerning how they meet internal and external customer needs are rarely overruled, leaving them to live with the consequences of their decisions.
- Commitment obsession. Since the market establishes the value of a company on the basis of its ability to create the value necessary to deliver on its earnings commitments, this discipline is instilled at all levels.
- Passion for learning. Legitimate mistakes are considered as a by-product of the decision-making process and are therefore viewed as learning experiences. 'Experience is the name everyone gives to their mistakes', as Oscar Wilde put it.

The VFE has mechanisms to protect itself against erroneous decisions, but it does not have a straitjacket labelled 'Gee I couldn't do that, it's more than my job's worth', impeding decision and robbing momentum at every level.

Has the CEO who says 'The buck stops here' ever reflected just how many times the buck has been passed before it reaches the desk bearing this legend? How much time this has cost? How many weakening compromise deals have been struck between employee and employee and department and department during the passing? What windows of opportunity have closed? In short, what value has been destroyed instead of created?

Organizations employing the VFE model don't draw their strength from some magic source. They create superior value by responding quickly to opportunity and making intelligent and informed decisions in the face of uncertainty. They also engender extremely high degrees of commitment, where people use creativity to solve problems and do whatever it takes to remove obstacles that might prevent value creation. Calculated risk taking is a distinctive feature where people play to win.

The VFE model can help establish alignment in your organization. Help you analyse the status quo. And furnish the objective insight necessary to do something about it. It should show you how capability gaps impede strategic execution. How to make your organization market relevant. And how to bring about alignment.

Capability gaps and unwritten rules sabotage value creation

Capability gaps? What are they? Well, when organizations fail to execute strategy, people are often viewed as the problem. Often they are. But they are not the problem behind the problem. To an outside observer (in an unaligned company that description may well include the CEO) the decisions and behavior of management and other employees who have failed to perform whatever actions were needed may seem irrational. However, these people were generally making logical responses to a flawed organizational model. The organization simply lacked the necessary capabilities to shape correct decision making.

The lookout on the *Titanic* didn't spot that passengers were shortly going to get more ice than their Manhattans strictly needed. Was his view unimpeded? The captain shouldn't have laid the ship's course so far south. Had the owners set too high a priority on the prize of the Blue Riband? The ship's architects had designed interior bulkheads that did not, in the event, prove watertight. Had the science of stress calculation proceeded far enough for them to have done so? You get the drift? People can only do what they are equipped to do.

Capability gaps can leave people ill-equipped to make complex decisions, leading them unwittingly to make inappropriate choices. While the resultant decisions may make sense for parts of an organization, the entity as a whole suffers. With the right tools, the impact of these incorrect decisions is often easily identified well in advance. What's more difficult to identify, however, is how capability gaps affect that crucial factor in 21st-century business, the speed at which decisions are made. It's no good doing the right thing if you do it too late.

Reflex speed of decision making all along the line is, above all, the attribute that governs how quickly, and therefore effectively, organizations are able to create appropriate value. But how can you assess this? Most organizations, like people, are not perfect. They will possess certain of the necessary capabilities in varying degrees of maturity.

Then there are unwritten rules. Experience shows that identifying an organization's 'unwritten rules' best exposes the impact of capability gaps. What are unwritten rules? Simply put, unwritten rules are hearsay evidence. The way people believe they must behave in order to be successful in an organization. They form over time to address capability gaps in unaligned organizations, or when aligned organizations initiate change without adding the necessary structures to maintain alignment. They are reinforced by what people observe and how they are rewarded, eventually becoming entrenched in the culture. Like hearsay evidence, they are unreliable and should not be admissible.

Organizations having similar characteristics and capability gaps generally exhibit similar unwritten rules. You know the kind of thing: people feel they need to be 'yes men' and, because they desperately want to avoid any association with failure, they wait out corporate change initiatives in case they go wrong. Which, of course, causes failure through lack of buy-in!

Unwritten rules impede strategy execution because they cause people to delay making decisions. Why do they do this? Wouldn't you if your job was on the line? People hold back on making a decision because they are afraid of making mistakes and losing position. Or they may hang fire because of political motives based on the display or acquisition of power. The extent to which unwritten rules delay decision making depends on the nature and size of the capability gaps. The larger the gaps, the more likely it is that decision making is being burdened by excessive political behavior.

Furthermore, unwritten rules are like Chinese Whispers. They may have started out, long ago, with some legitimacy. But they have been progressively distorted by being filtered through the perceptions and personal values of each recipient and onward communicator. Little wonder they end up working against value creation.

Organizations without the necessary capabilities are more likely to have problems allocating resources, adapting to change and executing projects. People will tend to have lower levels of commitment to executing strategy. Rather than having a 'playing to win' mindset, they are content to play to avoid losing. The consequences of these internal problems can be significant in terms of their effect on the loyalty both of employees and of customers. And on the value attached to the organization's shares by capital markets.

The key to addressing capability gaps is to understand how they are manifested in organizations. This will differ from one organization to another depending on just what rules no one has written down, and how people respond to them. Determining where and how they shape behaviour in general and decision making in particular is an essential first component of any programme intended to improve the organization's ability to create value and execute strategy. A later component is get those unwritten rules rescinded. Get them out of the company's mindset and processes. If Juliet had left a note, she and Romeo would have lived happily ever after.

Organizations need fluid internal communications, not to be confused with a function called 'internal communications' that send out missives, but a managed strategy with implementation processes and measures to assess how well the messages are being received, understood and acted upon.

We've got a great solution!
Where's the client?

Like Roy Orbison said, it's Gone, Gone, Gone. The existence of unwritten rules is often a sign that organizations are out of sync with the markets they are meant to be serving. Since their reflexes are slowed up by bindweed at every stage, how could they really be otherwise? They're still busy trying to implement the strategy before last when the strategy after next has passed its sell-by date.

Organizations that intend to maximize their value to customers and shareholders, not to mention stay alive, must be capable of taking their cues from market signals that are happening so fast they sound like white noise. Becoming market-relevant starts with the value proposition creation (as you have seen in earlier chapters). Market definition and segmentation is the first step in building a value proposition). From that flows customer value propositions and enabling activities. But they have to flow fast. The extent to which the outputs of an organization's activities meet customer expectations will ultimately determine the value realized. Therefore, how organizations delegate responsibility for these activities in the form of decision rights plays a central role in creating value.

A key component of establishing decision rights involves setting objectives that take into account the trade-offs associated with meeting customer requirements. There is no room or time in that process to take additional account of interdepartmental power squabbles or personal career angst. The service levels provided to customers must be balanced against their costs and the value they create for shareholders in both the long and short term.

The three-way trade-off between customer service, cost and shareholder value affects every aspect of the activities and outputs that comprise organizational performance. Reconciling the economics of these trade-offs at the business unit and customer levels (the benefits that will suit a particular customer circumstance, and what they are willing to pay in terms of money and risk, and the internal cost of providing the benefits) to the points where decisions are actually made is crucial. The ability to do it is a central purpose of the alignment contemplated by the VFE model. Internal delay at this stage is a value-depleting intruder that turns the deal into a four-way trade-off. Any enterprise that permits this isn't really serious about its markets or about doing business in the 21st century.

It is at the level of translation into business units that the elements of value-focused decision making are defined. For each activity, three questions must be addressed. What metrics best articulate the economics underlying the trade-offs? How can realistic targets for the trade-off metrics be agreed upon? What capabilities are required to encourage the right decisions and behaviors in calculating and negotiating the trade-offs?

Clear-eyed understanding of the economics underlying these trade-offs is even more critical at every decision point where several of an organization's units share resources. Companies must be capable of planning, measuring and reporting the component costs and profits of products and services provided to both internal and external customers. Moreover, they must be capable of doing so quickly. When organizations are incapable of doing this, resource allocation becomes more complex. Market signals become distorted. Decisions are made which result in cross-subsidization. Organizations become slow to react to changes in the market. Special studies become commonplace as they search for answers to dwindling margins, high overhead costs and excessive absorption of working capital.

Organizations employing the VFE model, on the other hand, are market-like in their thinking and actions. They know precisely how much each company unit is spending and how much it will return on spend. They allocate resources appropriately. Moreover, because organizational units have a natural ability to self-correct, they are not limited to the execution of strategy. They can shape it as well.

Orchestrating alignment – the way to value

Many companies have embarked on initiatives designed to achieve alignment. In fact, it would be difficult to find an organization that hasn't at least experimented with it. However, the list of organizations that believe such initiatives have created significant and sustainable value is a far shorter one.

Why do organizations that believe they have aligned their people and systems find it difficult to get value from the initiative? Simple. They're aligned on the wrong part of the target, addressing peripheral symptoms of corporate malaise instead of its central cause – aiming for the outer bands of the problem. Not the gold. Not focused on the one thing that above all others will ultimately deliver: the value proposition and the clarity it enables around decision making. Decisions are at the heart of every stage of everything that not only every company but every human being does every waking moment. So, unless an initiative changes the way people make decisions, realizing significant value from its implementation is unlikely.

Technological advances make this issue even more relevant today as organizations seek to improve decision making by more effective use of information. New technology provides the basis for fundamental changes in management process to establish as a VFE.

But technology is only a platform. Boston Symphony Hall has a great platform. But it's just 5,000 sq ft of Huntingdon Avenue real estate till the Boston Symphony Orchestra or the Boston Pops gets up there and gives. That's not at all a bad analogy. Up to 200 musicians, each making maybe a hundred or a thousand critical individual decisions during the four movements of a symphony, all these artists grouped in their separate orchestral sections under the guidance of a remote and elevated figure, interdependent upon one another, yet each entirely alone with the responsibility for making or marring a majestic piece of music, creating or destroying a transcendental experience for one-and-a-half-thousand people raptly attentive to every note. Alignment upon purpose of a barely imaginable order. Earlier, we mentioned Waterloo. The 1812 is a mere overture but, as an exercise in fully aligned, multiplex, purposive, real-time decision making, it rivals any half-hour of the actual event in Belgium on 18 June almost two centuries ago. And, boy does it deliver value.

Don't discount human nature

If you put around a table, the most gallant airman, the most courageous soldier, and the most stalwart sailor... you will get the sum of all their fears.

(Winston Churchill)

What distinguishes good leaders from great leaders is the extent to which their passion, their emotion, can be harnessed and used as a positive driving force throughout the entire organization. Think of the conductor of the Boston Symphony. He achieves alignment upon purpose of a barely imaginable order through engaging on an emotional level with each and every member of the orchestra. Without our human nature, our emotional nature, we will go through the motions, do as we are asked or told, but what really makes the task or job come alive is when we engage our whole selves – body, intellect and emotions.

There are libraries full of change programme case studies documenting examples of poorly managed, extremely costly new initiatives and programmes. There are also a number of management myths that surround this complex area of business evolution:

- The first management myth is that people in the organization will respond rationally and not emotionally to rational decision making and that this is normal in the world of work. The truth is our emotions always play the leading role. It takes a lot of effort for most people to stay coolly objective, and we can maintain our rationality for only limited stretches of time, and with the aid of tools and disciplines.
- The second management myth is that people are risk-averse and resist change. Actually, people are loss-averse. They translate this in such terms as: 'This means I'm going to have to do more work for the same pay', or, 'I'm about to lose my job'. If people's emotions as well as their intellect are engaged, they will actually embrace change, especially when they are enabled to see how they stand to gain or how they might avoid future loss.

So what is the best response to challenging business times? Well, managing the complexity of change and transition means it is absolutely essential to manage the change process caused by motives, thoughts and feelings for the benefit of the organization. Let's face it, without these things, people make up their own realities and spread discontent and misinformation.

Great leaders understand this and lead with their emotions. Great leaders also recognize the need to manage the human nature part of any change, any new initiative, as an integral part of the programme and not a bolted-on extra or afterthought (Figure 15.1).

The process of establishing the component capabilities of alignment is different for every organization. It depends on the maturity of existing capabilities, unwritten rules and the level of confidence and

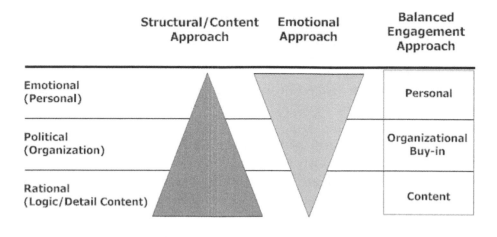

It takes 100% coverage in all 3 lanes to keep performance high during any organizational change.

Figure 15.1 The three layers of organizational change

trust people have in the management's ability to bring about change. Always, however, the chance of positive outcomes will be increased if: the change parameters are clearly defined; the impact of new capabilities on individual decision making is clearly defined; and unwritten rules are acknowledged and addressed.

Tackling these issues will help establish the level of commitment required to overcome inevitable obstacles, implement the sequential process of alignment and maximize its impact and the value you derive from it.

Darrell Jordan-Smith, vice-president, Global Communications and Media Industry at Sun Microsystems, Inc, makes the point that:

A properly defined and communicated value proposition is everywhere in evidence in a company. Right down to the individual. Our most successful sales people really understand this. Their personal value propositions are in alignment with those of the organization. These are the people who proactively work with experts inside Sun to produce value-creating solutions for our customers. These are the people who understand that Sun has an engineering heritage, and that they can get most value for our clients – and, in the process, for Sun – by involving technical experts in the solution-creating processes. So, actually, a value proposition has to be defined not only at the top level of a business, and at the sales opportunity level, and in terms of its application to individual target audiences within sales opportunities... but it has also to be defined for individuals within your own organization.

Where have we got to?
This looks like a new planet

We have moved from a world of mass production to one where goods and services can be provided on demand; from a 'Fordian' model offering any colour 'so long as it's black' to a spectacular rainbow of choices driven by customer demand; from an isolated, industrial economy to an networked, information society operating at exabyte speed. All of which makes for a more complex, more interconnected and more interactive business environment within which decisions have to be made, fast.

We are, for example, all accustomed to the fact that corporate teams now frequently operate on a seamless, time-shift basis every 24 hours – from the United States, to the Asia-Pacific, to Europe. More and more people are working in project teams where the work never stops – it just passes on to the next time zone.

The consequent outcomes are both exciting and daunting. Virtual teams may never physically meet one another. They may come from different cultures and speak different languages. And yet they must work seamlessly on the same projects, round the world and round the clock. This means, crucially, that they must all be aligned in terms of a common understanding of the value proposition that is the foundation of everything to which their organizations aspire.

Failure to achieve alignment could produce some apocalyptic outcomes. The size and longevity of a corporation, for example, is no longer any guarantee of continued survival. Increasing global interconnectivity means that the fleet of foot and mind can swoop on hitherto self-contained, 'safe' marketplaces. And those competitive threats may come from unexpected sources.

The danger here would be to hope that one-off adjustments, however radical they may seem at the time, will 'fix' the problem and equip an organization to march onward to an unassailable, profitable market space. Rather, there is the need to recognize that the new, continuously changing environment calls for equally continuous reassessment and adjustment. To thrive, organizations need now to be adaptable, flexible, responsive. It would be illogical, therefore, if they did not do everything in their power to nurture all of the potential brainpower, energy and enthusiasm already at their disposal, and make themselves attractive to more of the same. And yet, that is exactly what many organizations currently fail to do.

The value-focused enterprise recognizes this fact.

Join the debate? Discuss value propositions and the VFE further at www.valueproposition.biz

Note

1. Cisco Sees the Future, *Harvard Business Review*, November 2008.

Appendix A:
Back to the future

If you maybe think that our claim that customers have been second-class business citizens up until recently is untrue, here is how we arrived at it. We think this brief romp through nearly 200 years of the beat-up-on-the-customer model, selective as it inevitably is, makes the point.

> John Stuart Mill wrote that 'plausible pretence' was the characteristic of many people, and it had been forced upon them by demands of civilization. In a mass society, where individuals increasingly blended into a crowd, where universal rules of deportment took over from individualism and competition became ever more fierce, it was to be expected that there would be a prevalence of 'quackery' and 'puffing'. It was the unavoidable consequence 'of a state of society where any voice not pitched in an exaggerated key is lost in the hubbub. Success, in so crowded a field, depends not upon what a person is, but upon what he seems: mere marketable qualities become the object instead of substantial ones, and a man's labour and capital are expended less in doing than in persuading other men that he has done it.
>
> (*The Making of Victorian Values*, Ben Wilson, Penguin, 2007)

Early 19th century: customer misinformation – the hype of 'mere marketable qualities'

The quote within a quote above comes from a *London and Westminster Review* published in 1836, at a time of dizzying change in manufacturing, transportation and social conditions. Note the implied qualitative difference between 'mere marketable qualities' and 'substantial ones'. The idea of marketing as hype-laden customer con goes back, it seems, a long way!

Mid- to late 19th century: customer distraction – make trade, not war

In 1851, a seminal event: the Great Exhibition of the Works of Industry of All Nations, held in a gigantic iron and glass Crystal Palace covering 19 acres of London's Hyde Park. The six-month event, largely organized by Queen Victoria's consort Prince Albert, and attended by 6 million visitors, was a demonstration to the world of the pre-eminence of British industrial might... although the American exhibits of McCormick's agricultural machinery and Colt's revolvers were hugely popular.

The event was promoted as a showcase of world industrial ingenuity, but was actually intended to show that Britain was best, and to respond to a more subtle agenda. In her journal, Queen Victoria referred to 'my beloved husband, the creator of this peace festival'. A peace festival? Well, yes, because revolutionary ferment was in the air. A certain Karl Marx was convinced that the end of capitalism was imminent: after the failure of the 1848 uprisings Marx had argued that a new revolution was possible 'only in consequence of a new [economic] crisis', and he had been waiting impatiently ever since for the cataclysm to arrive. At Christmas 1851 he predicted that it 'must blow up at the latest next autumn... I am more than ever convinced that there will be no serious revolution without a trade crisis'.[1]

So, the Crystal Palace exhibition and subsequent trade fairs were political means to promote the maintenance of public order through consumerism: if customers could be mesmerized by industrial wonders, the logic went, they would be less inclined to upset the status quo. Make trade, not revolution!

It was a potent idea that the United States embraced in the aftermath of the American Civil War of 1861–65:

> The wealthy supporters of world's fairs were interested not only in showing off their private wealth but also in investing that wealth in a medium that they believed would help rebuild – literally reconstruct – the American nation after four years of bloody civil war. Inspired by the

nation-building examples of European exhibitions, they determined to use the medium of the world's fair to hasten the transformation of the recently reunited United States.[2]

The Philadelphia Centennial International Exhibition of 1876 was attended by around one-fifth of the entire US population of 46 million people.

Late 19th to early 20th century: customer enchantment – night becomes day

In 1879, Thomas Edison's invention of the light bulb changed the world. The light bulb:

> was a wondrous thing, but of not much practical use when no one had a socket to plug it into. Edison and his tireless workers had to design and build the entire system from scratch, from power stations to cheap and reliable wiring, to lamp-stands and switches... The first experimental power plant was built in two semi-derelict buildings on Pearl Street, lower Manhattan, and on 4 September 1882 Edison threw a switch that illuminated, if but faintly, 800 flickering bulbs all over southern Manhattan. With incredible speed electric lighting became the wonder of the age.[3]

As light bulbs turned night into day, shops and department stores grew in stature and appeal – Aladdin's caves of customer enchantment. These developments did, to an extent, achieve customer focus. In fact, Marshall Field, founder of the eponymous Chicago emporium, or his protégé Harry Gordon Selfridge, who subsequently founded the famous store on London's Oxford Street, are credited with coining the expression: 'The customer is always right'.

Early- to mid-20th century: customer manipulation – you are what you own

From the late 19th century, consumerism grew... until the Wall Street Crash of 1929 knocked the stuffing out of the markets.

Then, another seminal event occurred. Helping popularize Sigmund Freud's ideas in the United States, Edward Louis Bernays (1891–1995), the great man's nephew, came up with the idea that the consumption behaviour of the masses could be manipulated by appeals to their unconscious desires. This chimed perfectly with the identified needs of the US government: in part, the entrenched poverty of the 1930s was caused by their inability to control demand so that if only people could be persuaded to spend money, the economy would kick into action. Then, the logic went, if demand could be kept high, prosperity would be assured.

This marked the real birth of consumerism, in which demand, disconnected from need and channelled into desire, was deliberately stimulated in excess of the production and supply of goods. Semiology entered advertising. People bought fridges because any fridge was better than no fridge at all. You are what you own! The 'push economy' was born.

Second half of the 20th century: customer domination – producers and retailers rule

The period from 1945 to the 1990s was a golden age for producers and retailers. In particular, with industrial engines firing on all cylinders, the United States emerged from the Second World War in prime position to take advantage of market opportunities around the world, and big, multinational corporations burgeoned.

This was a period when might ruled. Established corporations could relatively easily keep control of resources, destroy nascent competitors before they were able to gain a foothold, and inexorably build market share. There were few communications channels, and they were expensive – so big players were able to dominate through mass advertising and promotion.

It was a time, too, when new ideas of organization and management emerged. For example, Alfred Sloane, president of General Motors, honed the idea of the departmental corporate organization, adding specialist units like marketing. Perhaps unsurprisingly, a great deal of post-war business organization followed a military model: hence, for example, sales forces with their sales targets, supported by marketing campaigns.

Concurrently, of course, huge technological developments were under way.

Mid-1990s onwards, and accelerating: customer power – finally, it's the customers' turn

In the 1990s things changed dramatically. The interconnected world was becoming a reality and a seminal work, *Reengineering the Corporation*,[4] showed the necessity to shift from the bureaucratically bloated, inwardly focused, vertically aligned organizations that that had grown to dominate marketplaces, to a lateral, customer-focused, process approach.

Virtually all enterprises, up to this point, adopted an inside-out view, manipulating the world to make things convenient for their own organization, departments and profitability. Now it became necessary to adopt an outside-in approach, changing the organization to meet the needs of its customers.

With an uncanny coincidence of timing, at the millennium, the old industrial order had keeled over stone dead.

This gallop through nearly two centuries of history is, of necessity, highly selective, but it surely makes the point that, right up to the late 20th century, the customer was accorded secondary consideration. The vested interests and sheer inertia to maintain a 'push' marketing and sales model throughout the 20th century proved irresistible.

Notes

1. *Marx's Das Kapital – A biography*, Francis Wheen, Atlantic Books, 2006.
2. *Fair America*, Robert W. Rydell, John E. Findling and Kimberley D. Pelle, Smithsonian Institution Press, 2000.
3. *Made in America*, Bill Bryson, Black Swan, 1994.
4. *Reengineering the Corporation – A manifesto for business revolution*, Michael Hammer and James Champy, HarperCollins, 1993.

Appendix B: Example value proposition for intel (partial)

Partially completed VP Template for Intel			
1 Who is the intended customer?	PC OEMs	PC retailers and resellers	PC end users
2 What will the customer's experience be of the offering and what price will they pay?	A well-supported quality product with well-funded global branding programme (Intel Inside) supported by an innovative global ecosystem enabling them to sell a new range of PCs profitably, with all of the power, speed and enhanced functionality that will delight retailers/ resellers and end users. The price is typically 10% higher than some competitor versions.	The capability to sell a new generation of PCs, profitably. These machines have all of the power, speed and enhanced functionality to delight end users – enabling true digital interconnectivity. Prices span all segments of the PC market except the lowest commoditized segment.	The capability to use all of the new multi-media resources that are emerging in the increasingly interconnected, collaborative digital world. The reliability, capability and performance justifies a 10% or more price premium.

		What will the customer's experience be of the company?	All of the historical/cultural track record of quality excellence from a continuous high-level commitment (up to 20% of revenue) to innovation through world-class R&D (the Tick-Tock product development strategy) – the reassurance of 'Intel Inside'. (We can demonstrate this by reference to the fact that Nehalem is in a sequence that will be followed by Westmere and Sandy Bridge.)		
3	What offerings will we create to deliver the intended experience to the intended customer? What purchase or usage of offerings do we want from the intended customer?	A new silicon process technology, embodied in a new category of products called Nehalem, that features twice the number of transistors of the previous chip, and runs on lower power.	A new generation of PCs with the Nehalem silicon process technology to enable more powerful PCs that will deliver the functionality that consumers need in order to be part of the emerging digital world, and will enable PC retailers to continue to operate on a profitable basis, delighting their customers.	The Nehalem architecture to power the reliable delivery of the most advanced internet applications, and services consistent with an accessible price ticket.	
4	What benefits will the customer derive from the experience and at what cost?	BENEFITS: The capability to create a new generation of PCs that will enable retailers/ resellers to flourish, and end users to access all of the current and emerging connectivity tools and applications. COST: Redesign and retooling for a new generation of machines.	BENEFITS: A new generation of PCs to attract existing and new end users, thereby helping ensure ongoing business. COST: Need to shift current inventory. Need to work with OEMs to market the new generation of PCs. Need to learn about/ train in the new capabilities of the new machines.	BENEFITS: The power and ability to run all of the current and emerging connectivity-based applications, including VoIP, IPTV and so on. Compact size and reduced power consumption. COST: The need to sacrifice the old machine. Premium price. The need to learn new applications that are enabled by the increased power.	

5	What competing alternatives do the customers have? How are we different?	Switch to different devices from alternative providers – eg subscription model via legacy and emerging service providers.	Switch to different devices from alternative providers – eg subscription model via legacy and emerging service providers.	Keep old machine, thereby saving money, disruption and uncertainty about new applications. Buy an alternative (probably cheaper) machine. Switch to another device (eg internet-enabled mobile phone, Netbook, etc).
6	How will we substantiate our ability to deliver the resulting customer experience measurably and specifically?			
7	Over what time frame will the proposition be delivered to the customer?	The new range will run for 2 years.	The range will sell for around 2 years.	A typical 5-year machine life.
8	How will the value proposition be communicated internally and externally?			
9	How will the value proposition be operationalized throughout the business?			
10	How will we measure and monitor the effectiveness of the proposition on our business?			

Index

Lightning Source UK Ltd.
Milton Keynes UK
UKOW06f0052250316

270869UK00012B/31/P